SIDEBAR

REFLECTIONS
OF A
PHILADELPHIA LAWYER

M. Kelly Tillery

Cover Photo: Independence Hall
          Philadelphia, PA
          ©Shutterstock
          Licensed

ISBN 13 - 9781721171439
ISBN 10 - 1721171436
CreateSpace Independent Publishing Platform
North Charleston, South Carolina

FOR MY FATHER

PREFACE

By 1985 I had been practicing law in Philadelphia for six years. While I had written a lengthy thesis in college, <u>The Armenian Non-Intervention: United States Relations With The Ottoman Empire, 1893-1897</u> (Swarthmore College, 1976), my subsequent works had been primarily rather dry legal briefs. That would change.

One wintry morning that year as I made my way through my daily stack of mail, I spied a small package from my Father. Putting aside reams of blue-backered pleadings I tore it open to find a slim, red, hardbound volume entitled <u>Well and Smartly Done – A Remembrance of War, 1943-1945</u> by Allen J. Tillery.[1] Abandoning the mail and canceling my morning appointments, I immersed myself in my Dad's tale of his 2 ½ years serving as a United States Marine interpreter on the bloody beaches and in the stinking jungles of several God-forsaken islands in the South Pacific in World War II fighting the Imperial Army of Japan.

In the first chapter of his work, Allen J. as I liked to call him in later years, says that he was inspired to write of his time "at the point" in war by his reading in high school of the Civil War experiences of his Grandfather, Milton Jared Tillery, C.S.A. (1834-1909) meticulously chronicled in the contemporaneous account of the leader of his unit, the W.P. Lane Rangers, W.W. Heartsill in <u>Fourteen Hundred and Ninety-One Days in the Confederate Army</u>. In 1965, twenty years after his discharge from 870 days in the United States Marine Corps, Allen J. wrote of his own coming to manhood in another great war.

To this day, I do not know why he let another score of years pass until 1985 before he shared his story. Nor can I account for why it took me yet another score of years until 2005 to write

---

[1] Now available on <u>Amazon.com</u>.

anything of a non-legal nature again. But Allen J.'s work inspired me to do so.

As a middle child, son of a lawyer and student of history, I have long had a passion for justice and equality. Within my family it earned me the tongue-in-cheek superhero nickname "VISORMAN," forever enshrined in a now infamous cartoon with follows drawn by my somewhat clever and artistic brother, Scott. Though the injustice references are dated, his point is clear.

These works were written between 2010 and early 2018 for publication in <u>The Philadelphia Lawyer</u>, the magazine of the Philadelphia Bar Association. Many were published therein and most others were approved by the Editorial Board for publication. Since <u>TPL</u> is a quarterly magazine, many may not have seen the light of day for some time. For that reason and because several of my supportive colleagues on the Board have urged me to share with a larger and more diverse audience, this volume contains some of my works written for <u>TPL</u> in those years, but not yet published. Some may know me for my articles and presentations on Lincoln. Those are not included herein as they will soon be published in another book next year.

The reflections, musings, polemics and, some may say, rantings which follow are meant to make the reader contemplate and, if moved, to act against injustices wherever encountered.

Peace,

M. Kelly Tillery
June, 2018
Philadelphia, Pennsylvania

TABLE OF CONTENTS

VII. **THE CLOWN**

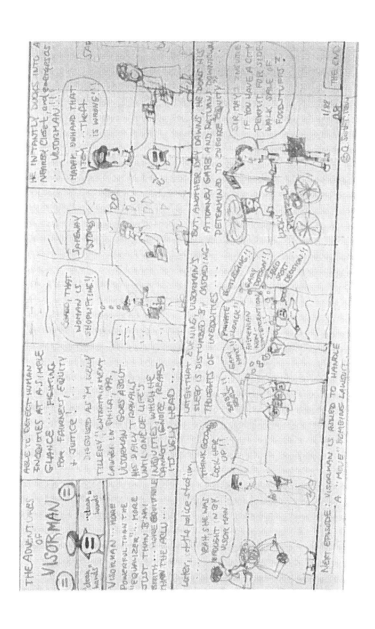

"The Adventures of Visorman" – A. Scott Tillery
©1988

I. TILTING AT WINDMILLS

"YOU CAN FIGHT CITY HALL – THE CASE OF THE POPE'S PLATFORM"[2]

Thirty years ago this month, on September 12, 1979, as I just settled into my new apartment at The Dorchester, I watched Mayor Frank L. Rizzo proudly announce on the evening news that Pope John Paul II would visit Philadelphia, and that the city was already constructing a huge cylindrical platform over Logan Square, where the Pope would celebrate Mass. Viewers with a sense of history, and irony, might have been reminded of another Pope, in another time, also on a platform – Pope Urban II, who from a "lofty platform in the midst of an open plain" at the Council of Clermont in Auvergne, November 27, 1095, appealed to his bishops to start what would become the First Crusade.

I, however, as a recent graduate of the University of Pennsylvania Law School, awaiting my bar exam results and about to join a venerable Philadelphia law firm, was simply stunned. How could this be? While perhaps not the most serious joining of church and state since the conversion of Constantine, I knew that this undertaking struck at the heart of the fundamental principle embodied in the Establishment Clause of the First Amendment – separation of church and state. I had studied all of the U.S. Supreme Court First Amendment cases, and this was an obvious violation of the Establishment Clause. And it had to be stopped. Not the Pope's Mass, of course, just taxpayers paying for it.

I spent the balance of that evening drafting a federal lawsuit against the City of Philadelphia and showed up on the doorstep of the American Civil Liberties Union first thing the next morning with a draft complaint in hand. Hilda Silverman, Executive Director of the ACLU, concurred with my analysis and the ACLU took the case.

---

[2] The Philadelphia Lawyer, Vol. 74, No. 4, Winter 2010. The Philadelphia Lawyer is the quarterly magazine of the Philadelphia Bar Association. The author is a member of the Editorial Board and a former Editor-In-Chief.

Later that same day, I slipped quietly into an official city press conference featuring a bevy of self-important officials, including City Commissioner of Public Property Robert Silver, City Managing Director Hillel S. Levinson, City Representative Joseph A. LaSala and even the city's chief legal officer, City Solicitor Sheldon L. Albert, all of whom positively beamed and strutted announcing that hard-earned taxpayers' monies would be and were being used as they spoke to design, plan and construct the Pope's Platform, where he would celebrate a solemn and sacred Roman Catholic religious ceremony.

A classic display of the arrogance of power. I could not believe what I was hearing and seeing. Was the academic world I had left only a few months before so divorced from this reality? I looked around for Rod Serling.

Since I was not yet a member of the bar (my admission would not come until October 11, 1979, just 8 days after the Pope's Mass), I could not handle the case as a lawyer. Although I considered serving as plaintiff, I soon discovered that the law firm I was to join had very close ties to Mayor Rizzo, so suing the City of Philadelphia was probably not a good career move.

However, I had set this train in motion and there was no stopping it. The ACLU soon found a plaintiff taxpayer, Susan Jane B. Gilfillin, and veteran First Amendment litigator Henry W. Sawyer, III, and suit was filed seeking a temporary restraining order and preliminary injunction. But, the parties, based upon representations from a non-party, the Archdiocese of Philadelphia, agreed that if the court ruled in favor of the plaintiff, the Archdiocese would reimburse the city for any unconstitutionally-expended funds. Construction of the "Pope's Platform" continued unabated, and the Pope celebrated Mass without incident on October 3, 1979, on top of a beautiful $200,000 + platform paid for, at least initially, by the taxpayers of Philadelphia. Frankly, I thought this temporary "compromise" was unwise, unnecessary and constitutionally impermissible. But what did I know? I was not even a lawyer yet.

In my naïveté, I actually believed that since the legal issues were so clear and obvious that the city would "do the right thing" and either not construct The Platform with taxpayers' dollars or require someone else, such the Archdiocese, to pay for it. Boy, was I wrong. Rather than do the constitutionally proper thing, the unflappable Mayor Rizzo spent hundreds of thousands of dollars in time, legal fees and other costs defending this lawsuit in the U.S.District Court and the U.S. Court of Appeals for the Third Circuit, both of which ruled against the city, finding that this amounted to "public sponsorship of a religious service" and that $205,569 in taxpayers' money was expended unconstitutionally to build, in essence, an outdoor church (with 30' high cross!) for the Pope to celebrate Mass. *Gilfillan v. City of Philadelphia*, 480 F.Supp. 1161 (E.D.PA. 1979) *affirmed* 637 F.2d 924 (3rd Cir. 1980).

Fortunately, the federal courts stood as a bulwark against the ill- advised actions of this rogue mayor, ruling against the city's disingenuous and sophistic arguments, finding that the "religious effect" of these expenditures was "both plain and primary" and, as such, violated the First Amendment.

The First Amendment is not only numerically first, it is first among equals in substantive import. As originally proposed, it was the third of 12 amendments, but became "the First" when the First Congress failed to ratify the first two. The "Establishment Clause" of the First Amendment is actually the first prohibition of six contained therein and provides that "Congress shall make no law respecting an establishment of religion, ..." By the Fourteenth Amendment, it applies to the states and to political subdivisions such as the City of Philadelphia. Curiously, the particular language as enacted came not from the pen of any of the famous Framers who felt strongly about this issue such as James Madison, Patrick Henry or Thomas Jefferson, but rather from an early legislative vehicle of compromise – the Congressional Joint Committee.

As Leonard W. Levy says in his scholarly work, *Origins of The Bill of Rights*, "Above all, the establishment clause functions to protect religion from government, and government from religion."

U.S. District Judge Raymond J. Broderick stated the issue before him simply as: "… whether or not the Constitution of the United States permits the expenditure of public funds by the City for the construction and preparation of the platform which served as a base for the altar used by the Pope and the clergy in the celebration of the Mass before approximately one million people assembled at Logan Circle." My Philadelphia-born and raised Yankee wife tells me his law clerk was obviously not from the city, as locals know it is really Logan Square.

Judge Broderick ruled that the Constitution did not permit these acts and the U.S. Court of Appeals for the Third Circuit agreed. The Archdiocese of Philadelphia, as it had agreed to do in the beginning of the case if the city lost, reimbursed the city (the taxpayers) $205,569, purportedly the amount of the unconstitutional expenditures. The city actually spent over $1.2 million in connection with the Pope's visit, but went to great, and sometimes absurd lengths to except certain expenditures as allegedly not directly related to the Mass. As with the TRO "compromise," I also thought it unwise and wrong to leave unchallenged many of these expenditures and claims that some items were "not related" or "reusable." But again, I was unprepared to disagree with the ACLU's lead counsel who had successfully argued First Amendment cases in the U.S. Supreme Court.

The city argued that The Platform was for the security of "an international dignitary and head of state," the safety of the crowd and to maximize access and visibility for all who wished to see and hear the Pontiff. On appeal, "creative" city lawyers even came up with a fourth, new "reason", not argued earlier, that the money was for a "public relations bonanza" for the city. Although Judge Broderick went out of his way to say that "The Court does not question the sincerity of the city's expressed reasons", many scoffed at these belated and apparently pretextual arguments. The Third Circuit was less kind, calling the city's arguments "transparent", "imaginative", having "no merit" or "only superficial appeal", and "only partially true."

It is true that popes, on occasion, since as early as 882 when John VIII was beaten to death (albeit by his own entourage), have, on occasion, been targets of assassins. This Pope, John Paul II, himself was victim of such an attempt less than two years after his Philadelphia visit, which was the genesis of the oddly eponymous "Popemobile." For those diehards, however, tempted to say, "I told you so," the Third Circuit Court of Appeals cogently observed "… the Pope's position on the platform made him a clear target in any direction."

Judge Broderick wisely found that the city's acts (1) amounted to public sponsorship of a religious service, (2) had the primary effect of advancing religion, (3) fostered an excessive entanglement of government with religion, of two types – (a) joint participation in the planning of and preparation for a religious function, and (b) promotion of divisiveness among and between religious groups, thus failing not one (which alone would have doomed the acts), but all three of the U.S. Supreme Court tests to determine a violation of the Establishment Clause.

Amazingly, the city engaged in yet additional unconstitutional activity after the case was filed, when it ordered The Platform left standing for more than a week to let Philadelphians visit it and, as the Third Circuit said, "… thus created a temporary shrine" – "activity not compatible with the Constitution."

It is interesting to note that the Pope also visited our nation's Capital that same month and said an outdoor Mass for hundreds of thousands on a $400,000 platform. That platform was, however, paid for by the Washington Archdiocese, not the city government and without the need for litigation.

The City of Philadelphia compounded its boneheaded decision to pay for The Platform with the decision to fight relentlessly for the right to compel taxpayers to pay for it, first in the district court and against in the appellate court. The city surely spent more litigating this loser of a case than it spent on The Platform. With thanks to heaven for little favors, city taxpayers were finally delivered from the unconstitutional burden of the costs of Rizzo's Crusade, when the U.S. Supreme Court denied the City's Petition for Certiorari.

I am no longer so naïve to believe that other elected officials may not in the future choose so audaciously to flaunt constitutional imperatives such as the Establishment Clause. I do, however, believe that these important court decisions make them think twice in this regard. The Mayor of Philadelphia foolishly wasted an enormous amount of taxpayer dollars in disputing a clear legal position and was chastised by the judiciary entirely appropriately.

Thirty years later, most of the players in this constitutional drama have passed this veil of tears. Pope John Paul II, Mayor Frank L. Rizzo, District Court Judge Raymond J. Broderick, Henry W. Sawyer, III, City Solicitors, Sheldon L. Albert and Alan J. Davis and Hilda Silverman, are all no longer with us. But the First Amendment lives on. And *Gilfillan v. City of Philadelphia* remains good law.

As for me, I passed the bar and built a career protecting the intellectual property rights of a wide variety of clients, including, perhaps ironically, Madonna, Black Sabbath and The Grateful Dead.

Although I am Jesuit-educated and sometimes ribbed for having "sued the Pope" (not precisely true), I am pleased and proud that I was able to play a small part in preventing a serious violation of a very important part of the First Amendment to the United States Constitution. We fought the good fight. We fought City Hall and we won.

"GET OFF LIVINGSTON AVENUE"[3]

From the time I could consciously reason, my father, a Louisiana country lawyer in the mold of Atticus Finch, curiously counselled me to "Get off Livingston Avenue." We lived on that "Avenue," in reality, an unadorned suburban development street, grandiloquently named after Robert R. Livingston (1746-1813), first U.S. Secretary of Foreign Affairs and Jefferson's Minister to France who negotiated the Louisiana Purchase, of which this eponymous roadway is a part-a fact no one who lived there knew then or probably knows now. I looked it up in our World Book Encyclopedia (pre-Google) when I was 12 and "got off Livingston Avenue" five years later.

I now sit high above one of the five squares of William Penn's Greene Towne in a corner office at the storied mahogany partners' desk of Senator George Wharton Pepper (1867-1961), founder and scion of the 124 year old Philadelphia law firm at which I am now a partner. Exactly 1,220 miles "off of Livingston Avenue." Although my father often muses that he never meant for me to get that far off, he knows not that the Philadelphia Bar of 2014 is actually light years and eons away from the world in which I was born and bred.

I left the Deep South, not only because of the adventures my parental prodding promised, but also because it was, as H.L. Mencken so appropriately denominated, "The Sahara of the Bozart" (1920) and, because of the pervasive stench of racism. In 1978, I spent half the summer working for a prominent, large New Orleans law firm to determine whether I should to return the prodigal son to take advantage of my roots, family resources and connections. At a summer clerk luncheon, a firm senior partner answered that question for me when he told a "joke" utilizing the "N-word" and all but a few laughed heartily. I was sickened and

---

[3]The Philadelphia Lawyer, Vol. 77, No. 3, Fall 2014

told my father that night that I would never practice law in Louisiana or return to Livingston Avenue.

I am eternally grateful to my parents and others for giving this barefooted boy from the bayou so many extraordinary opportunities which enabled me to become a "Philadelphia Lawyer." Opportunities that millions of other of my era did not have solely because they were different, most because they were of a different race, the race of the millions of Americans enslaved for 256 years and subjected to Jim Crow and worse for another 100. Those that believe that the Civil Rights Laws of the 1960's, Affirmative Action and a black President have created a level playing field of equality of opportunity, much less of actual equality are, at best, ill-informed.

Two recent books read will change forever the way you view race in this country: Slavery by Another Name – the Re-Enslavement of Black Americans from the Civil War to World War II, Douglas A. Blackmon (Anchor Books, 2009 – Pulitzer Prize Winner) and When Affirmative Action Was White: An Untold History of Racial Equality in Twentieth-Century America, Ira Katznelson (W.W. Norton & Co., 2006). Though freed from actual slavery on December 6, 1865 by the Thirteenth Amendment, blacks endured disenfranchisement, the KKK, Jim Crow, legislative and judicial indifference and abuse, and perhaps most importantly, from 1932-1965 an almost absolute exclusion from the government largesse of The New Deal, The Fair Deal, and The New Frontier.

My father came back from World War II and rose from poverty to the great white middleclass , going to college and law school and buying his first home courtesy of the G.I. Bill of Rights. Although 1 million African-American served in WW II, few received any of the horn of plenty that was the G.I. Bill.

I would not be where I am without Affirmative Action, that afforded my parents, but also a more direct version. Though a Caucasian male, I was admitted to Swarthmore College, one of the most exclusive colleges in the nation, not because of my brilliance or stellar academic record, but primarily because I was from the backwaters of Louisiana and seemed to have promise. The

G.I. Bill and fortuity of birth and geographic diversity created my window of opportunity.

I often tell young men and women considering our profession, including my own children, that there are too many lawyers in this country (the most per capita of any nation), but there are still not enough good ones.

The American Lawyer, June 2014, article "What's Wrong With This Picture?" chronicling the lack of diversity in large law firms is filled with startling and disturbing statistics showing that our profession has not changed as much as we may have thought or hoped. Ferguson, MO, is not the only evidence of the persistent and festering sore of racial prejudice and inequality in our society.

It is my hope that in my role as Editor-in-Chief of this magazine, I shall, in some small way be able to enhance and encourage opportunities for others of different races, cultures, backgrounds, faiths, sexes, sexual orientation and origin, in their own Jeffersonian "pursuit of happiness." And, if that includes becoming a Philadelphia Lawyer, so much the better.

This magazine is considering doing what it has never, in its 77 year history, done – devote an entire issue to one theme - "Race and Law."

I treasure and trumpet diversity, not primarily as reparation for past injustices and inequality, though a noble goal in and of itself, but rather as an incredible vehicle to achieve the best results for us in our practices, our firms, our communities and our world. We have not even come close to realizing the Jeffersonian goal of a government securing certain unalienable rights, including life, liberty and the pursuit of happiness to all men who are created equal. We have much to do.

"UNDER SIEGE"[4]

Democracy is under siege in this nation. Not by ISIS, Khorasan, Al Qaeda, the Taliban, Ebola or Putin. Rather by an insidious domestic threat as serious as the internecine war which 150 years ago tested whether this nation or any nation conceived in liberty and dedicated to the proposition that all men are created equal could long endure.

Fortunately, this nation did endure that challenge to our democracy. At an astonishing price in blood and treasure. While that threat to the foundation of the Republic was as open and blunt as possible, the modern equivalent is much more subtle, clever and thus, nefarious.

Some say that the infection of our electoral process by Big (and Dark) Money permitted by Citizens United v. FEC, 558 U.S. 310 (2010) or the relentless systematic Gerrymandering of Congressional Districts permitted by Vieth v. Jubelirer, 541 U.S. 947 (2004) alone or together are the greatest dangers to our sacred democracy. While each in its own way is reprehensible, and part of a larger, well-organized effort to prevent as many people as possible from voting one way, the most abhorrent threat is the nationwide effort to directly actually disenfranchise eligible voters. The most fundamental right in a democracy – the right to vote is, for millions, in grave danger.

Our history includes stunning examples of substantial enfranchisement, all by Constitutional Amendment remedying past disenfranchisements based upon certain criteria – XV Amendment (1870) – "color, race, or condition of servitude"; XIX Amendment (1920) – "sex," and XXVI Amendment (1971) – "age" (18 years or older). And, of course, the XXIV Amendment (1964) which prevented disenfranchisement "by reason of failure to pay any poll tax or other tax." Each was required, along with scores of enabling acts and judicial decisions, because our system, while paying lip

---

[4] The Philadelphia Lawyer, Vol. 77, No. 4, Winter 2015

service to universal suffrage, has from its inception been undermined by a never-ending series of legal and extra-legal schemes to prevent certain groups from voting.

Not coincidentally, my own first effort to cast a ballot, here in Pennsylvania, met with the arcane and cumbersome laws designed to prevent young, liberal students from voting. I turned 18, voter-eligible, just a month before the 1972 McGovern-Nixon Presidential contest wherein the war in Vietnam was the central issue. Because I had resided in Pennsylvania for less than 90 days, I was caught between the parochial absentee voting requirements of my state of origin, Louisiana, and the restrictive residential requirements of my new home state, Pennsylvania. At the polls in Swarthmore, some haughty, blue-haired matron coldly told me I could go to Court in Media, try to convince a Judge that I should be able to vote, get an Order and come back and maybe the polls would still be open. In my then naiveté, I actually thought Pennsylvania might be different than Louisiana. Not so much. I would have preferred a Literacy Test or a Poll Tax.

Modern voter suppression, dilution and disenfranchisement takes many and varied forms, all of which fit, however, into five categories (1) voter identification requirements, (2) time and location restrictions, (3) attacks on voter registration, (4) "purging" voter rolls, and (5) barring felons from voting. Not to mention, also blocking meaningful Immigration Reform. The Disenfranchisers are as relentless as they are creative in finding new ways to legislate disenfranchisement. And, yes, they are here in the Commonwealth of Pennsylvania.

In 2008 a divided (6-3) U.S. Supreme Court upheld an Indiana voter suppression law requiring government-issued photo identification at the polls, holding that "evenhanded restrictions" protecting the "integrity and reliability of the electoral process itself" pass Constitutional muster. Crawford v. Marion County Election Board, 553 U.S. 181 (2008). At least 16 states have such requirements and more are planned. It should not be surprising that this same "facially neutral" reasoning was used often by the Court over 100 years earlier to uphold a variety of legal disenfranchising statutes. And in 2013, an even more divided Court (5-4), led by the new Four Horsemen (Roberts, Scalia, Thomas and Alito), emasculated The Voting Rights Act of 1965 reaching the tone deaf conclusion that 'things had changed dramatically' and thus there was no longer a need for the Federal Government to approve voter restrictions in Southern states. Shelby County v. Holder, 557 U.S. 193 (2013) Au contraire, mes amis.

While litigation will always be an avenue to challenge the Disenfranchisers, we obviously cannot rely upon the courts alone to protect our democratic system. This battle must also be fought at the state legislative level and, more importantly, in the Court of Public Opinion. Frankly, we need to turn public opinion on this issue with the same astounding speed and thoroughness with which it has so recently changed on marriage equality.

If those pressing voter restrictions really believed in democracy and universal suffrage, they would instead enact laws designed to enfranchise, to encourage people to vote and to make it easier to do so. The truth is, of course, obvious – they do not want more people to vote because they fear, and rightfully so, that new and certain vulnerable groups of voters will not vote as they wish.

However, recent history teaches that the current electorate may not be quite as passionate about voting as I or our forebears. In the recent mid-term elections, only 36% of eligible voters voted. Which means about 19% of eligible voters determined the political fate of the nation for at least the next two years. And at least half of that 19% vote against their own economic interest being either deceived or distracted by the shiny objects of fear and extraneous emotional social issues. So, our "democracy" runs on the will of less than 10% of the electorate? Perhaps we get the government we deserve.

Lest you think this well-funded, comprehensive, coordinated national campaign of voter suppression could not possibly be successful in this country, see the U.S. Supreme Court's October 18, 2014 Order in Veasey v. Perry (No. 14A393 and 14A404) which permitted Texas' Voter I.D. law to take effect for the mid-term election – shades of things to come. The purported justification for Voter I.D., the most recent and pernicious suppression weapon, is to prevent in-person polling place fraud. Yet nowhere in the legislative histories, court records, academic studies, government studies, court opinions or briefs has anyone produced any evidence of even one case of such fraud. Ever. Not one. As Tova A. Wang, author of The Politics of Voter Suppression, (Cornell University Press 2012), says, it "is an invented problem," in effect, itself a fraud.

And, keep in mind, that the progenitors of today's Disenfranchisers, Southern Senators, Congressmen and State Legislators, by 1911 had repealed virtually all state and federal Reconstruction-era election laws and enacted literacy tests, poll taxes, property tests, understanding tests, the white primary, grandfather clauses, stringent residency requirements and inconvenient places and times for registration and voting, (everything but "Voter I.D." – a relatively recent, creative suppression tool), disenfranchising every black voter who had been enfranchised less than 50 years before by the XV Amendment. It would take another 50 years and the passage of the XXIV Amendment (1964) and The Voting Rights Act (1965) to begin to reverse these legal obscenities.

Although the Disenfranchisers shamelessly pretend to have the noble purpose of protecting the integrity of the process, all but the most blind and dense, including a few Supreme Court Justices, do not see (or wish to see) through this ruse. However, as with so many on the wrong side of history, technology will overrun them. Secure online voting systems will one day enable every eligible voter to vote easily. We are quite creative when we want to be. The first Patent of our most prolific inventor, Thomas Edison, was for an electromagnetic voting machine. (June 1, 1869, U.S. Pat. No. 90646A). We do virtually everything else online and there is no reason why we cannot devise and implement secure online voting systems which will finally make universal suffrage and democracy a reality in this country and end the disingenuous efforts of a powerful few to silence the votes of the powerless many.

Canada, Sweden, Switzerland, Latvia and Estonia have all had excellent experience with online voting. As we take pains to protect the Baltic States from the Russian Bear, perhaps we can also learn something from them and enfranchise millions via new technology. Right after we join the rest of the world (except also Liberia and Myanamar) and adopt the metric system.

"SOUNDS OF SILENCE"[5]

In the last quarter century, the Philadelphia Bar Association Board of Governors has passed about 500 resolutions, some of which concern issues beyond our profession. The most recent supporting action on climate change, is a good example. Others concern such issues as land mines (against), diversity (for), marriage equality (for), bullying (against), religious freedom (for), and discrimination against women (against).

Some view resolutions as worthless pontification which only placate liberal consciences. Lincoln hesitated to issue an Emancipation Proclamation until he could give it effect, telling a group of ministers on September 8, 1862, "I do not want to issue a document that the world will see must necessarily be inoperative, like the Pope's Bull against the comet." In 1456, Pope Calixtus III supposedly had issued a Papal Bull ordering Halley's Comet not to appear in the sky. Lincoln issued his Preliminary Proclamation two weeks later. Covering 3 million slaves, the final Proclamation of January 1, 1863, had actually freed over 1.3 million by late 1864. And the 13th Amendment, ending slavery, was born of two crusading women, Elizabeth Cady Stanton and Susan B. Anthony, who began a petition drive, just 2 ½ years before it was adopted 150 years ago, this December 6th.

It occurred to me that because our Association had existed for 63 years during which slavery was legal, including in Pennsylvania until 1848, perhaps it had spoken on this seminal national scourge. Unfortunately, neither our nor any other bar group ever said anything about slavery. Or about the 13th Amendment. Nor did any speak out on any other major social or political issue of the day.

To be fair, antebellum bar associations were more like exclusive social or library clubs and protective professional guilds, not having the wider mission such as that of ours today, "to

---

[5] The Philadelphia Lawyer, Vol. 78, No. 2, Summer 2015

serve the profession and the public by promoting justice, professional excellence and respect for the rule of law and … strive to foster understanding of, involvement in and access to the justice system."

Trained lawyers did not arrive here until after the English "Glorious Revolution" of 1688. Parliament's Bill of Rights (1689) inspired some English lawyers to spread the good word of "rights" to the colonies, though not to those then here enslaved

Ours is the oldest continuous bar association in the U.S. (1802). Detroit, Cincinnati and New Orleans had bar associations, as did six slave states, though, similarly, not one seems to have spoken on slavery, at least not against it.

There is, however, ample evidence of individual members of this bar who bravely spoke out and litigated cases which helped erode and bring about the eventual demise of the slave power.

Philadelphians William Rawle (1759-1836) and David Paul Brown (1795-1872) were two of the earliest and bravest lawyer-abolitionists who spoke out vociferously and often against slavery, despite the unpopularity of the cause and substantial risk to their own safety and livelihood.

Philadelphia jurist John Meredith Read's (1797-1874) public stance against slavery expansion cost him a seat on the Supreme Court when President Tyler withdrew his nomination in 1845 due to Southern opposition.

In 1851 Philadelphia lawyers Read, Brown, Theodore Cuyler, Joseph J. Lewis, and W. Arthur Jackson secured acquittal of a white miller in the celebrated treason trial arising out of the Christiana Riot in which a large group of blacks and whites prevented the U.S. Marshal from capturing a fugitive slave.

Other Philadelphia lawyers such as Horace Binney (1779-1852), Jared Reed Ingersoll (1786-1868), John Sergeant (1779-1852), Evan Lewis (1782-1834), George H. Earle, Sr. (1823-

1907), and William Morris Meredith (1799-1873) were publicly active in opposition to slavery.

And at least 5 of our first 6 Chancellors, acting as individuals, strongly and publicly opposed slavery. The second, Peter S. DuPonceau, (1760-1844) spoke out, but against abolitionism, not slavery.

The silence of some such as Chief Justice Benjamin Chew (1722-1810), John Dickenson (1732-1808) and even the first "Philadelphia Lawyer," Andrew Hamilton (1676-1741), may be, in part, because they each owned slaves.

In 1860, there were 33,193 lawyers in the U.S. (no women, only 4 black), 2,414 of whom in Pennsylvania. Only a handful spoke out. And an even smaller number took action.

There is no record of any lawyer amongst the 2,000 settlers of Jamestown, Virginia on August 20, 1619 when "20 and Odd Negroes," slaves from Angola, first arrived on a Dutch ship. And there is no record of anyone objecting on that day or any day for a long while thereafter.

This, the first time slavery was brought to mainland America, was the crucial opportunity for someone to speak out and say, "No!" What a different world we might live in if just one person, particularly one political, business, religious, or legal leader, had had the guts to say, "No. Not here!"

There also arose no hue and cry from any Philadelphians, lawyers or not, in 1684 when the British ship Isabella offloaded the first 150 African slaves on our Delaware River docks. Most were purchased by Quakers at auction at the London Coffee House at the southeast corner of Front and High (now Market) Streets, a frequent gathering place for members of the bar.

Ninety years later, Thomas Paine (not a lawyer), who for a time lived across the street, was one of the first to speak out in his first essay, "African Slavery in America" (March 8, 1775).

Great public apologies began in 1077 when Henry IV apologized to Pope Gregory VII for political conflicts with the church, but there has been an explosion in the last 25 years. The U.S. has apologized for internment of innocent Japanese Americans in WWII and doing ghastly experiments on African-Americans at Tuskegee Institute, but it has never apologized for slavery.

The Senate (2009) and House (2008) passed different apology resolutions but, unsurprisingly, could never agree on common language. President Clinton expressed regret for the slave trade (1998), but there has never been a formal government apology.

Some say apologies are as useless as resolutions. But perhaps it is time for the nation to do so. And, perhaps for our Association as well, for not standing up and saying, "NO!" as its first act, in 1802.

Of course, no officer or member of ours or any association pre-1865 lives today. But that is likewise true of officers, directors, employees, stockholders and leaders and citizens of entities which have apologized for involvement in and shared responsibility for slavery.

In the last decade, numerous disparate entities have apologized, including the City of London, Ghana, Benin, Wachovia, J.P. Morgan, Aetna, and Lehman Brothers.

In 2005, Philadelphia enacted a law requiring those doing business with the City to research and disclose any historical ties to slavery, though not mere silence in the face of it. Lest you think these corporate mea culpas were a result of the soul-searching of repentant executives, know that most were a result of a similar 2003 Chicago ordinance.

But this is not about slavery. Or apologies. It is about silence. In the face of injustice.

John Stuart Mill's "marketplace of ideas" cannot produce truth, wisdom, and effective solutions unless and until we actually come to market and ascend the soapbox.

Whether we heed Eldridge Cleaver, "If you're not part of the solution, you're part of the problem," Albert Einstein, "If I were to remain silent, I'd be guilty of complicity," Martin Luther King, Jr., "In the end we will not remember the words of our enemies, but the silence of our friends," or Paul Simon, the sounds of silence speak volumes.

As members of the bar, we are privileged to have special powers which come with heavy responsibility, not only to our clients, but also to our community, nation and planet. If we remain silent, we fail.

"ON DECLARING WAR"[6]

"The Congress shall have the Power . . .
To declare War, . . ."

U.S. Constitution
Article I, Section 8, Clause
11, September 17, 1787

"The Constitution supposes,
what the history of all
governments demonstrates,
that the Executive is the
branch of power most
interested in war, and most
prone to it. It has
accordingly with studied care
vested the question of war to
the Legislature."

James Madison To
Thomas Jefferson, 1798

One need not harken back to Korea or Vietnam to study modern U.S. military interventions, for in just the last quarter century, we have intervened in Kosovo, Bosnia, Afghanistan, Iraq, Libya and most recently, Syria. All without Congressional Declaration of War. Since the end of WWII, we have expended over two trillion tax dollars and killed and maimed hundreds of thousands of our own and other nations' citizens in a myriad of underclared wars.

Seventy-four years ago, on June 5, 1942, Congress anti-climactically last exercised its exclusive constitutional power to declare war – on the hapless Axis nations of Bulgaria, Hungary and Romania. In the ensuing years, this nation's armed services have

---

[6] The Philadelphia Lawyer, Vol. 79, No. 4, Winter 2016

been engaged in active combat against others virtually every minute of every day – all without Declaration of War.

Congress has declared war only eleven times, in five wars – The War of 1812 (United Kingdom), The Mexican-American War (Republic of Mexico), The Spanish-American War (Spain), World War I (Germany and Austria-Hungary) and World War II (Japan, Germany, Italy, Bulgaria, Hungary and Romania). Yet, in at least 129 other instances, a president authorized military action in and/or against another nation or people without securing (or even seeking) Congressional Declaration of War. What is to explain these repeated, apparently unconstitutional, acts of our chief executives, both Republican and Democrat?

CONGRESSIONAL WAR POWERS

While the Constitution gives Congress alone the power to "declare war," it also grants Congress at least ten other specific war powers: (1) to provide for the common defense; (2) to define and punish piracies and felonies committed on the high seas, and offenses against the law of nations; (3) to grant letters of marque and reprisal; (4) to make rules concerning captures on land and water; (5) to raise and support armies; (6) to provide and maintain a navy; (7) to maintain rules for the government and regulation of the land and naval forces; (8) to provide for calling forth the militia to execute the laws of the Union, suppress insurrections and repel invasions; (9) to provide for organizing, army and disciplining the militia, and for governing such part of them as may be employed in the service of the United States; (10) to prevent any state, without Congress' consent, from keeping troops, or ships of war in times of peace, . . . or engage in war, unless actually invaded, or in such imminent danger as will not admit a delay. (Article I, Section 8)

In light of these awesome Congressional war powers, and the actual and frequent war-making of presidents since Jefferson, sans declaration, bested the Barbary Pirates in 1803, one might expect to find a similar, if not greater, litany of war powers specifically bestowed on the President under Article II.

Au contraire, mes amis. Article II provides <u>only</u> that (1) the executive power is vested in the President; (2) the President shall take an oath to "faithfully execute the office of President of the United States, and will to the best of his [my] ability, preserve, protect and defend the Constitution of the United States; (3) the President shall be Commander in Chief of the Army and Navy of the United States; and (4) he shall have the power, by and with the advice and consent of the Senate, to make treaties.

That's it. And frankly, the real "war power," or at least that claimed by president after president is based only upon three words "Commander in Chief." Never has so much power based upon so few words affected so many. At least in a democracy.

QUAINT AND ARCHAIC?

Has the Congressional power to declare war become just a quaint, archaic, chivalrous notion not to be taken seriously in modern times? Sure, the Constitution has some musty old provisions – when is the last time Congress granted Letters of Marque and Reprisal (1815, actually), or tried to "work corruption of blood" or quarter soldiers in any house, etc.? But, are these of the same magnitude and import as the breath-taking authority to declare war?

The only other such significant Constitutional provision which has fallen into similar desuetude is the "advice" portion of the Senate's "advice and consent" limit on the Presidential power to make treaties. Washington took this provision seriously when in August of 1789 he brought Secretary of War Knox's treaty with the Creek Nation to the Senate. In sincere effort to seek the Senate's "advice," the Father of our Country was so disgusted with his treatment by the first Senate that he resolved never to meet with them again. And with that unilateral, precedent-setting decision, Senatorial treaty "advice" was forever read out of the Constitution. No President ever again sought the "advice" of the Senate on a treaty.

ACTUAL DECLARATIONS

An examination of the eleven Declarations reveals several interesting and common elements and some not so. The first three were "Acts" of Congress, the latter nine "Joint Resolutions." A distinction without a difference, perhaps, as all passed, though requiring only a majority, most by more than two-thirds majority of each House. All were signed into "law" by the President.

Curiously, in light of the tension between the President and Congress in this realm, each specifically provides that it "hereby authorizes and directs" or "directs and empowers" the President to use "the entire land and Naval forces" of the United States to "carry on the war" and the last nine say specifically "to bring the conflict to a successful termination." If the "Commander in Chief" already had such power, why, one wonders, did Congress need to vote a Declaration to "authorize and direct" him?

With the 1917 Declaration against Germany, Congress settled on a template (drafted by some unheralded State Department functionary) of three simple paragraphs: (1) the actual Declaration; (2) a "WHEREAS" clause referencing unspecified "acts of war" committed by the enemy; and (3) the authorization of the President to use U.S. forces to carry on the war and to bring it to a "successful conclusion."

None specify the actual "acts of war" perpetrated, how the President is to use our forces, or what would constitute a "successful conclusion." However, each was preceded by a Presidential request for same, which included a recitation of the "acts of war" justifying a declaration, including some evidence thereof. In the last five, Congress acknowledged that the offending nation had declared war on the U.S. first. Presidents and Congress often, if not always, attempted to present the public with the acts purporting to justify "war", some of the evidence thereof, the military plan and the goals for the peace.

Each declared war was ended by treaty negotiated by the President, using his Constitutional power and "consented" to by the Senate (no "advice"), by at least the required two-thirds vote.

It is curious that the Constitution requires a majority of both houses of Congress to declare war, but only a two-thirds majority of one house to end one, at least, if, as is common, done by treaty. As Constitutional Convention Delegate Oliver Ellsworth (Conn.) opined, "It should be more easy to get out of war than to get into it."

So, each Declaration was (1) requested by the President, (2) passed by at least a majority of both houses, (3) authorized the President to use military forces to "carry on" war, (4) identified the particular enemy nation, (5) directed the President to use forces toward a "successful termination," and (6) limited authorization from the date thereof to a "successful termination." A simple, clear and accountable method to declare war.

"AUTHORIZATIONS FOR USE OF FORCE"

Some politicians, scholars, courts and pundits argue that a Declaration is not required to commence hostilities, as long as there is a Congressional "authorization" (and funding) - the "functional equivalent" thereto. Though, if that were so, Article I, Section 8, Clause 11 would seem superfluous.

In addition to the eleven formal Declarations, Congress has passed and the President signed and implemented, coincidentally, another eleven "Authorizations of Use of Force" – from the first in 1798 for the "Quasi-War" with France, to the last for Iraq (2002). Congress and the President have used this euphemistic vehicle to make war, even though there is no provision for same in the Constitution. Each does all that a Declaration does except actually "declare" that a "state of war" exists between the U.S. and the nation (or other) against which military forces are to be used.

Congress issued eleven Authorizations: 1798 – France – twice; 1802 - Regency of Tripoli; 1815 - Regency of Algiers; 1955 – to protect Formosa and The Pescadores; 1957 - to protect any nation in the Middle East against armed aggression from any Communist country; 1964 - North Vietnam; 1983 - Lebanon – removal of all "foreign forces;" 1991 – Iraq ("Persian Gulf War"); 2001 - "those responsible for the recent attacks of 9/11"; and 2002 – Iraq, again/still.

Each Authorization and Declaration names another sovereign nation as the enemy, except four Authorizations. The first of which, in 1819, authorized the President to attack and seize unspecified "pirates" in the Caribbean who had been preying on U.S. commercial vessels. The second, in 1957, authorized President Eisenhower to assist any nation in the Middle East threatened by "overt armed aggression from any nation controlled by International Communism." The third, in 1982, authorized President Reagan to utilize U.S. forces in a peacekeeping effort which specified no particular enemies in Lebanon, a nation then filled with a wide variety of local and foreign armed military personnel. And the last, in 2001, authorized President Bush, to use military action against unspecified nations, organizations or persons that he determines "planned, authorized, committed, or aided the terrorist attacks that occurred on September 11, 2001," the most unprecedented and incredibly broad authority ever granted to any President. And that worked out so well.

Yet what of the other 129 or so uses of military forces in and against other nations by presidents, without any Congressional authorization, much less any request for same, essentially, instances of presidents following the old saw, "better to beg forgiveness (or ratification/funding), than to ask permission." Is that really what the Constitution provides? Or what The Framers intended? And do we or should we care?

"JOINT RESOLUTION CONCERNING THE WAR POWERS OF CONGRESS AND THE PRESIDENT"

Better late than never, several months <u>after</u> the last U.S. troops left Vietnam, on November 7, 1973, Congress attempted to reassert its war powers, passing, over Nixon's unsurprising veto, "The War Powers Resolution," providing that a President can send armed forces into action abroad <u>only</u> by Congressional authorization <u>or</u> if the U.S. is already under attack or serious threat. And, most importantly, limiting the action to 60 days (with a 30 day withdrawal period), <u>unless</u> there is a Congressional Declaration of War <u>or</u> Authorization of Use of Force.

Some say this is an unconstitutional delegation of Congress' powers to the President, while others suppose it an unconstitutional limit on the President's powers as Commander in Chief.

James Madison, Father of the Constitution, reported in his semi-official record of the Constitutional Convention of 1787, that the phrase "<u>make</u> war" was changed to "<u>declare</u> war," so that the President would have the power to repel sudden attacks, but <u>not</u> to commence war without explicit approval of Congress.

"THE MOUSE THAT ROARED"

At times, others have declared war on the United States and we did not deign to respond in kind. In March 1801, the Barbary State of Tripoli declared war on the United States and seized American commercial ships. Though a "strict constructionist" himself, reluctant to act without a Declaration of War, Thomas Jefferson, based not on a Congressional "Declaration," but on a "grant of authority" to use all means to defeat the Tripoli pirates, did so with a vengeance, resulting in a Treaty of Peace and Commerce in June, 1805.

Again, in 1815 the Regency of Algiers, not learning the lesson imposed by U.S. Marines on "the shores of Tripoli" ten years earlier, also declared war on the United States. This time,

President Madison requested a Declaration, but Congress refused to grant same - the only time where a president requested a Declaration and Congress refused. Fortunately for Madison and the protection of United States commerce, Congress gave him everything but a formal declaration and the Bey of Algiers regretted it the rest of his life.

One might also count the May 6, 1861 Confederate States of America's Congressional Declaration of War on the United States as the third non-response. Jefferson Davis called Lincoln's April 15, 1861 "Proclamation Calling Militia and Convening Congress" a Declaration of War on the Confederacy but strictly speaking, it was not. Although Congress did declare that a "state of hostilities" existed, Lincoln ignored the Rebel Declaration, as responding in kind would have given the traitors recognition as a nation, something Lincoln and his Republican-controlled Congress eschewed in almost every respect.

And, most recently, in 1998, Osama Bin Laden and Al Qaeda declared war on the U.S. While ignoring him to our peril, we did rather informally "declare war" eventually (and oddly), not on him or Al Qaeda, but on their tactics – "terror." And we all know how well that worked out for Osama.

WHY NOT DECLARE WAR?

So, why does Congress not just declare war when it is believed necessary to commit our armed forces to combat? First, that would require, at least by tradition, that a specific enemy be identified, with articulated justifications, with overwhelming evidence of bad acts of the enemy, and with specific goals for termination. That exercise necessarily brings public scrutiny, debate, disagreement and ultimately accountability. Not things of which politicians are particularly fond.

Second, a formal declaration, by virtue of existing statutes, automatically activates at least 150 provisions requiring a wide variety of federal agencies to take very specific, burdensome, expensive and accountable actions.

WHO'S NEXT?

Flush with the adrenaline of our "success" in Libya (2011), we were called upon to support the Arab Spring in an area including at least 14 more authoritarian governments, all ripe for overthrow and/or democracy and capitalism. Then there is Africa, South and Central America or the Far East where we also find scores of such governments. And even more recently, to stamp out new insurgents/terrorists with curious names such as ISIS/ISIL, Khorosan, Boko Haram, etc. What's an International Policeman to do?

Although candidate and constitutional law professor Obama opined in 2007 that the President does not have the Constitutional power to use military action that does not involve an actual, imminent threat, President Obama proudly proclaimed in 2011 that he, and he alone, decided to commit military forces against the Libyan military. Apparently, however, he had a change of heart when it came to bombing Syria in 2013, requesting Congressional authorization. And again in November 2014, asking Congress for authorization to use force against ISIS in Iraq and Syria, though, curiously, 6 months after he already had done so. Perhaps he was influenced by the 2008 bipartisan National War Powers Commission which recommended requiring the President to consult with Congress before using force. Nevertheless, Congress has failed to act and seems unlikely to do so anytime soon.

The Framers did not intend to give this choice, by whim or caprice, to our presidents. Madison must be rolling over in his grave.

WHY CARE?

As members of the bar, we took a solemn oath, just like Members of Congress, the President and all Federal Judges, to uphold the U.S. Constitution, the entire Constitution.

A Declaration of War requires the body politic and our leaders to think about, articulate, evaluate and declare the evidence for, reasons for, and goals of war, thus ensuring justification, accountability, certainty and an endgame. The Declaration of Independence was really our first and it set forth both rather nicely.

Our latest, largest undeclared war, in Iraq, is the poster child for the principle embodied in this constitutional provision. George W. Bush's "reasons" morphed over time from Al Qaeda's responsibility for 9/11 (no evidence) to Weapons of Mass Destruction (none found), to Democracy (not there yet), to Oil For Food (what?), to end of Tyranny (not yet). And today, astoundingly, he still says his was "the right decision."

Perhaps if we required, as the Founders did, an actual Congressional Declaration of War we would make war less often or when we do with an actual evidentiary basis therefore and clearly stated goals.

"JUST ONE VOTE"

My youngest turned 18 today and I placed her voter registration form in the mail just as the sun rose. I smiled wistfully, thinking of one of my favorite college political science professors, the brilliant James R. Kurth, who shocked my innocent liberal classmates and me in 1974 by telling us that he had never voted. And never would. Because, he said, his vote would never make any difference.

On its face, of course, he was probably entirely correct. My mother and father sometimes chose not to vote in presidential elections, agreeing that their votes would cancel each other out. It reminds me, however painfully, that my vote, or that of new voter, Katie Tillery, is equal to that of any one of those tiki torch marchers in Charlottesville. (U.S. Constitution, Amendment XXVI)

While I know that President Andrew Johnson was impeached, but avoided conviction in the Senate by one vote, and that the ad hoc commission that decided the 1876 presidential election gave it to Rutherford B. Hayes over Samuel Tilden by one vote and, of course, that the U.S. Supreme Court gave the 2000 presidential election to George W. Bush over Al Gore when it stopped the Florida recount by one vote, I did not know whether there were any actual, verifiable historical incidents to show Professor Kurth wrong, or at least in doubt, that is, that any popular election, at any significant level, was decided by one vote.

CLOSE, BUT NO CIGAR

First, it seems that there have been as many as 174 popular, modern elections which have been very close, that is, decided by a margin of less than 0.1%, including a 2016 Pennsylvania State House Race (Dist. 31) in which Perry Warren (D) defeated Ryan Gallagher (R) by 28 votes out of 37,936 cast (.07381%).

Second, the number actually decided by just one vote seems to be rather small, by my rather unscientific count, something like 16, some as long ago as 1887 and the most recent just last year. While 10 of those are, curiously, Canadian federal elections (eh?), three were in U.S. state races, New York (1910), Alaska (2008) and one in Virginia just last year (2017).

One of the earliest and perhaps most famous was lawyer Marcus "Landslide" Morton, who was elected Governor of Massachusetts in 1839. By one vote (51,034 to 51,033).

TIES ... THAT BIND

In 2015, Mississippi lawyer, Mark Tullos (R) tied farmer, incumbent Blaine ("Bo") Eaton (D) in a contest for the Mississippi State House District 79 seat. Each got 4,589 votes. So, as Southern gentlemen often do, they drew straws to determine the winner. Lawyer Tullos drew the shorter green straw. Mr. Eaton returned to his seat in the House and Mr. Tullos to his country law practice. Democracy was safe in the Magnolia State. However, Mr. Tullos ran again in 2016 and defeated Mr. Eaton. Touché.

Just recently, Shelly Simonds (D) at first appeared to defeat incumbent Virginia House of Delegates member (94th Dist.) David Yancey (R) by one vote (11,608 to 11,607) making that body evenly divided 50 Democrats and 50 Republicans. Such an even party balance has never happened in the 400 year history of that august legislative body. And, there was no official procedure for breaking any inevitable tie vote. A recount produced a tie and a drawing was suggested. Yancey's name was pulled from a film canister out of a ceramic bowl, giving the Republicans a one vote majority. But, inevitably, a court challenge has followed.

So, Professor Kurth, these unicorns do exist!

Popular culture (i.e., the Internet) is filled with bad, false misinformation about everything, including, unsurprisingly, a lot of canards about famous "one vote margin" elections - none of which will be repeated here, so as not to inadvertently perpetuate any. Suffice it to say that if we stray from general elections to representatives bodies, the incidence of one vote victories (and defeats) increases substantially and requires a more select focus on issues of great import.

In the beginning, although the 1787 Philadelphia Convention was called by the Confederation Congress "for the sole and express purpose of revision of the Articles of Confederation," in its first substantive vote, the Convention voted, in complete contravention of its mandate, to repudiate the Articles. By one vote (6-5). Politicians failing to heed their own directives – what an auspicious and telling beginning. Soon thereafter, they voted to apportion representation in the House and Senate. By one vote (6-5). But then they changed their minds, at least as to the Senate, via the Connecticut Compromise. You guessed it. By one vote (5-4).

Constitutional amendments are not immune to this phenomenon. On August 18, 1920, Tennessee's Legislature passed the proposed 19th Amendment, finally giving women the vote, becoming the 36th state to ratify it and making it official. By one vote (49-48). Twenty-four year old Republican State Representative Harry T. Burn changed his vote, breaking a tie, fittingly because his mama wrote a note to him to be a good boy and vote for "women's rats to vote."

The most comprehensive study, done by Casey B. Mulligan and Charles G. Hunter in 2001, examined over 56,000 U.S. State and Congressional elections since 1898. Of those, only seven state legislative and one congressional election were decided by one vote. "The Empirical Frequency of a Pivotal Vote," Public Choice, 2003, V.116.

While this phenomenon is curious, it surely is not so that it should be the deciding factor, one way or the other, as to whether one should actually take the time and expend the energy to vote in any election. And, likewise, in the realm of voting, it should be one of our least concerns.

What should concern us all, to our core, is low voter turnout, voter suppression, and Gerrymandering. Then there is Russian meddling and/or collusion, but that is a whole other issue. Low turnout, suppression and Gerrymandering are things that we as individual citizens and voters can actually do something about.

SHAMEFUL

Only a little more than half of the eligible voters actually voted in the 2016 Presidential election (56.9%). Belgium turns out 87%, and 57 other nations also best the U.S. in turnout. Sad fact for the world's first modern and oldest democracy. Perhaps we actually get the government we deserve, if we allow 28.45% of all eligible voters to decide who governs.

ALSO, SHAMEFUL

The principle of "one person, one vote" has been firmly established in our jurisprudence since the Supreme Court ruled in Reynolds v. Sims 377 U.S 533 (1964) that state legislative districts must contain roughly the same number of people.

Elbridge Gerry, statesman, diplomat, and our 5th Vice President, had a stellar career, but sadly is known primarily for the redistricting plan he implemented as Governor of Massachusetts in 1812 to keep his Republican Party in power, giving birth to the monstrous "Gerry-mander" and an enduring and infamous political concept. By the way, his name is pronounced with a hard "g," though over time that has morphed into a soft "j."

It is, of course, not without irony that the modern Republican Party (though not descendent from Gerry's) has become master of the Gerrymander to retain power, drawing districts that resemble alien beasts unimaginable even to the clever politicians of the founding era. The courts will have final say, however. The Pennsylvania Supreme Court in a 5-2 decision just struck down the Republican Gerrymandered Congressional District map and three similar challenges are now before the U.S. Supreme Court.

EVEN MORE SHAMEFUL

Enemies of democracy have long and often devised clever ways to suppress the vote of those with whom they do not agree. Sometimes it is simply by violence and/or threat of violence, but the most insidious and effective in our time is by law. Whether sex, race, age, or property qualifications, poll tax, literacy test, roll purges, or voter ID, the products of the fertile minds of the vote suppressers seem to know no bounds. The latest farce, the "Presidential Commission on Election Integrity" claims to seek out evidence of widespread voter fraud. Or so says The Siberian Candidate. At least he did, before he dissolved his own commission. Can the "Presidential Commission on Fairies and Unicorns" be far behind?

The great thing about democracy is periodic elections. We get another chance. And even if there is only a one in 60 million chance that the average voter will decide a race, we cannot afford to take the risk of not voting. Have you read the news lately?

Your vote is your free pass to complain until the next election. If you choose not to take it, perhaps you should remain silent until you do vote. Fewer than 40% of people on this planet live where voting even exists, and in many places the franchise is quite limited. Be grateful for your right.

It may very well be that in my lifetime, no election in which I am eligible to vote will be decided by one vote, but, if the unthinkable ever happened, and I did not vote, I would never be able to face my Katie again.

Thus, we have both committed to vote in every election in which we are eligible. What about you and yours?

**   PROFESSOR KURTH REPLIES:

"Dear Kelly,

I apologize for replying very belatedly to your engaging letter of August 22, but I have been traveling and thus away from the office of the Political Science Department at Swarthmore. Thus, it was only now that I have received and read your letter. (You may have thought that I had not replied because I was annoyed, but, as you will see, my response has been just the opposite. I have been delighted and indeed edified by your wonderful letter and article.)

There is definitive proof that on the matter of "just one vote" you are right today, and that Professor Kurth was wrong in 1974. That proof is that Professor Kurth, who "had never voted. And never would," started to vote in 1992 and has voted in every election since. By that time, several good reasons for voting had accumulated in the mind of Professor Kurth. However, the decisive one was a version of the reason that you give near the end of your article:

"Your vote is your free pass to complain until the next election. If you choose not to take it, maybe you should remain silent until you do vote."

By 1992, I had many good friends who were in a variety of serious and useful occupations, professions, or simple life situations, which were utterly unlike the rather rarified and esoteric field of "political science" (such as it is). Whereas fellow political scientists might think that my rarified and esoteric arguments for not voting were rather clever and bemusing, my other friends were more inclined to think that, on the matter of voting at least, I was either a lunatic or moral monster. Since I did like these friends and I did enjoy complaining until the next election, I started to vote (and to complain) in the 1992 election, and I have thoroughly enjoyed the experience ever since. I highly recommend it to others.

I also thoroughly enjoyed many other parts of your article. I was especially pleased and edified to meet all those unicorns. Of these, the most wonderful was "lawyer Marcus 'Landslide' Morton, who was elected Governor of Massachusetts in 1839. By one vote."

You can feel free to share this testimony of my miraculous conversion experience to anyone that choose.

Warm regards and best wishes,

James Kurth
Swarthmore College"

"OF MONUMENTS AND MEN"[7]

The Fifth Circuit Court of Appeals, sitting in New Orleans, recently ruled that the City of New Orleans may remove from prominent public display long-standing statues of Confederate States of America President Jefferson Davis and Confederate Generals Robert E. Lee and Pierre Gustave Touton Beauregard.

I rode by those statues on my way to school every day for 13 years, often wondering why the City so honored racist traitors. My Father, a lawyer, Civil War buff, and grandson of a Confederate cavalry veteran, tried to explain that it was just "part of our heritage."

I did not buy that then and still do not.

IN THE BEGINNING ...

Americans have a legacy of removing statuary of detested leaders, a legacy that began even before the Republic was formed. On July 9, 1776, the first public reading of the Declaration of Independence in New York City inspired the citizenry to pull down the equestrian statue of King George III in Bowling Green park. It had been commissioned and erected only six years earlier to commemorate the King's "beneficence" in repealing the Stamp Act. The irony of honoring an unelected monarch for repealing his own onerous enactment in the face of potential rebellion was never lost on the incipient patriots. Made of lead, the decapitated remains were converted into 42,088 musket balls which the Continental Army soon put to good use against the real King George's Redcoats in the name of liberty. Recycling at its earliest and best.

Curiously, a new replica of that George III statue, produced by Studio EIS of Brooklyn, serves as the centerpiece of a historical tableau at our new Museum of the American Revolution which opened on April 19, 2017.

---

[7] The Philadelphia Lawyer, Vol. 80, No. 3, Fall 2017

In the earliest known removal of a Confederate name, in 1862, "Jefferson Davis" was removed by Lincoln's Department of the Interior from the granite memorial honoring the builders of the Union Arch Bridge, an engineering marvel and part of the Washington Aqueduct.

STATUE TOPPLINGS

Repugnant public statues have often been toppled rather suddenly and unceremoniously throughout history. Most such topplings have been conducted by either revolutionary mobs, victorious opponents in war, or new leaders erasing evidence of their predecessors. Modern monument removals, however, are different – most often the result of a deliberate, thoughtful, democratic process having the noble goal of preserving history while not honoring the archaic and reprehensible.

Some argue that monument removals are an effort to rewrite, conceal, or erase our history or heritage. On the contrary, removal advocates fully intend that no one ever forget the subjects, their acts, or the events. With, of course, a different focus. They are not to be remembered or honored for their "accomplishments," "character," or "greatness," but rather, precisely the opposite.

COMMEMORATE WHAT AND WHY?

Modern, transparent, inclusive bodies tasked with considering removal, whether they be private, academic, or governmental, all wrestle with the same question – by what standards or criteria do we judge existing monuments erected in the past, most often by and for persons who no longer exist. Before addressing the criteria by which we might determine whether any monument should be removed, we should first be clear on why such monuments were erected in the first place and continue to be maintained and what present purposes, if any, they purport to and actually serve.

First, let us limit this inquiry to monuments owned and maintained by governmental entities on public display on public land. If you desired to erect a statute of Hitler in the privacy of your backyard, not visible to the public, while appalling, public outcry for removal would probably be limited.

Second, we are apparently a people obsessed with monuments. There are 1,328 on the Gettysburg Battlefield. The Pennsylvania Historical and Museum Commission Historical Marker program receives over 50 applications annually, though it approves only about one-third of them. At present, there are over 2,000 such markers throughout our 67 counties. Philadelphia tops the list with 244. My personal favorite is a privately-placed plaque on a Society Hill building which reads: "On this site in 1897 absolutely nothing happened."

Third, these are admittedly political, not legal, decisions. As the Fifth Circuit observed:

> "Finally, we note the limited scope of our judicial review. We do not pass on the wisdom of this local legislature's policy determination, nor do we suggest how states and their respective political subdivisions should or should not memorialize, preserve, and acknowledge their distinct histories. Wise or unwise, the ultimate determination made here, by all accounts, followed a robust democratic process." Monumental Task Committee, Inc. v. Chao, No. 16-30107, March 8, 2017.

Most statues or monuments were/are erected to "commemorate" and/or "celebrate" a notable person, action or event. Note the relevant definitions:

"MONUMENT"

"A structure, edifice or erection intended to commemorate a notable person, action or event.
OED, Vol. XI, p. 1045, Def. 4a

"COMMEMORATE"

"To call to remembrance, or preserve in memory, by some solemnity or celebration."
OED, Vol. III, p. 545, Def. 2

"CELEBRATE"

"To speak the praises of, extol, publish the fame of."
OED, Vol. II, p. 1018, Def. 5

In the not so distant past, large public statues and monuments were erected to educate and remind the citizenry of great men, accomplishments, and events. In the current era of 90% literacy, 84% internet access, 96% television access, 1300+ daily newspapers and 1,000,000+ new books published annually, every citizen now has ready access to facts and figures about any person, accomplishment, or event worth noting for any reason, good or bad. Thus, the need for such public erections is not what it once was.

THE CRESCENT CITY FOUR

The New Orleans Robert E. Lee Monument was dedicated on Washington's Birthday in 1884. In attendance were Jefferson Davis and P.G.T. Beauregard themselves, as well as thousands of Confederate veterans. The New York Times noted the irony calling Lee "the greatest of those who drew his sword to destroy what Washington created." An 1877 City Ordinance stated that the grounds were "dedicated to the memory of General Robert E. Lee." Although funded, erected, and donated to the City by the private Robert E. Lee Monumental Association, it was placed on City-owned park property and maintained by the City.

Without a 16.5' statue on a 60' pillar, does anyone really think we might have forgotten the man who dishonored his oath, turned traitor on his nation, and led a war machine for four years to destroy the Union and save slavery? Bobby Lee, as Lincoln often called him, was not a one-hit wonder.

The Jefferson Davis Monument was dedicated in 1908 with prominent Kentucky lawyer and former C.S.A. Lieutenant Bennett H. Young, the principal speaker, claiming that the monument would "speak through coming ages to the world of the Southland's love and appreciation of the life and character of Jefferson Davis." Young was the post-war leader of the "Lost Cause" movement. The Davis statue was paid for and erected, in part, by the private Jefferson Davis Monumental Association, but also with some state funding, and placed on City-owned park land. On the pedestal is engraved: "His name is enshrined in the hearts of the people for whom he suffered, and his deeds are forever wedded to immortality." Jefferson Davis' "character" and his "deeds"? Really? Where do I start?

The P.G.T. Beauregard Equestrian Statue was dedicated in 1915 and may present a more difficult case. While the "Little Creole" was a prominent Confederate general and commanded the attack on Fort Sumter that started the Civil War, he was also, in the post-war era, a powerful and effective advocate for reconciliation. Perhaps it would be different if Beauregard were not dressed in full CSA General regalia and sword astride his war horse. The Beauregard Monument Association, a private group, raised most of the necessary funds, but the City and State also contributed, and the City Park Commission donated the land.

A fourth, the "Battle of Liberty Place" Monument, the subject of a separate, subsequent court decision, is probably the easiest to evaluate for potential removal. New Orleans Mayor Mitch Landrieu has called it "the most offensive." The 35-foot-tall obelisk was erected by the City in 1891 and placed prominently at the foot of Canal Street, to commemorate the three-day traitorous, racially-motivated 1874 insurrection by the Crescent City White League paramilitary against city police and state militia of the

Reconstruction state government. And the City went further in 1932, adding a plaque praising the battle's role in re-establishing "white supremacy."

Removed due to road construction in 1989, it remained "in storage" until 1993, when David Duke, former Grand Wizard of the KKK, sued for its return. In compromise, the City returned it to public display, but to an obscure location in a curve in Iberville Street, between railroad tracks and the entrance to a parking garage. And the City replaced the 1932 plaque with one commemorating police casualties, some of whom were African-American.

Davis, Lee, and Beauregard were traitors who fought a war killing 750,000 and maiming twice as many to maintain and expand the most reprehensible institution known to man. They clearly present a distinct class – different in degree and kind.

When it comes to those who "simply" owned slaves, one has to conduct a more nuanced analysis – how many, for how long, under what circumstances, at what age acquired, any manumission – in life or at death, etc. And, equally important, one must include in the balance the positive accomplishments of the person being remembered. For example, though slave owners, Washington and Jefferson have considerably more positive weight on the historical scale in their favor than, say, Supreme Court Chief Justice Roger Taney or John C. Calhoun.

"TAKE 'EM DOWN"

New Orleans is a unique American city with an almost 300 year history of racial, ethnic and cultural diversity and inclusion. Yet, despite this, it remains one of our most racially divided cities. As is often said, "it is a great city to be from and to visit, but not to live in." But the perfect crucible for forging new ideas.

It is also a city rich in symbols. And those monuments are powerful symbols. As Federal District Court Judge

Carl J. Barbier said in his opinion allowing the removal of the "Battle of Liberty Place" obelisk, "…monuments on public property typically represent governmental speech." (citing <u>Pleasant Grove City, Utah v. Summum</u>, 555 U.S. 460, 470 (2009). So, if these symbols are constant public statements by the City government, just what is it that they are intended to communicate and, perhaps more importantly, what do they actually communicate?

The history of each makes pretty clear what was intended to be communicated at the time of their installation. And the City has made clear what it <u>now</u> intends to communicate by their removal. As Judge Barbier also said, "the City has a right to speak for itself."

The self-appointed defenders of the offensive statuary rather vaguely claimed, at least in the case of the Liberty Place monument, that its purpose today was to "recognize conflicts that emerged in New Orleans and elsewhere during the post-Civil War period." A rather neutral, lawyer-like, facially unoffensive purpose.

But, obviously, it does so much more and, in so many ways. The "Take 'Em Down NOLA Coalition" (takeemdownnola.org) argues that such public displays are all offensive government-sponsored symbols of white supremacy, then and now, and were erected when blacks were denied the vote by Jim Crow. If I was offended when I rode by them as a child, how do young black children feel when they do now? These activists further argue that the monuments misrepresent the community, compel the very folks oppressed to pay taxes to maintain them and demean and psychologically terrorize the black community. None of the "defenders" addressed these points, at least not in legal filings.

<u>NOT ALONE</u>

We are hardly the only nation to face these difficult decisions. While we cringe when the Taliban and ISIS destroy priceless ancient statues, some men no doubt much less praiseworthy than Confederate generals or slave owners, we cheer when statues of Stalin, Lenin, and Saddam Hussein are toppled.

In the United Kingdom, controversies rage over statues of men from Cecil Rhodes to General Arthur "Bomber" Harris. And in a reverse controversy, the Japanese government is working assiduously to get the South Korean government to remove statues of Korean "Comfort Women" in Seoul and Busan, because they cause remembrance of Japan's reprehensible acts in World War II enslaving thousands of Korean women as sex slaves for the Japanese Imperial Army.

And the controversies extend further into our past. Christopher Columbus statues and monuments, including the one on our Delaware Riverfront, have been the subject of removal demands due to his mistreatment and enslavement of indigenous peoples. Pepperdine University relocated its Columbus statue, to a less hostile location, its campus in Florence, Italy.

The Huffington Post recently ran a hilarious satirical piece about President Trump calling for the removal of the Statue of Liberty "because it encourages immigration." Why, Trump asks, would we invite and welcome the "tired, poor, huddled masses and wretched refuse"? If they were all Eastern European supermodels, it might be different.

THE PUBLIC FISC

New Orleans had to assure the Federal Court that it would use only the finest, most experienced experts to remove the monuments so they would not be damaged. But as many in the South are so oddly fond of saying, "the war ain't really over." The first removal contractor hired by the City backed out after his car was torched.

And, indeed, to mollify opponents, the City also had to promise that the monuments would again be displayed somewhere else, presumably in a less prominent location in something like an elephant's graveyard of embarrassing statuary. The City already has dozens of creepy actual graveyards as well as many equally haunting warehouses of old Mardi Gras floats. Rumor has it that they may return as exhibits of shame, not honor, in a Slavery Museum.

Which brings us to the extraordinary expense of removal, storage, and re-display. Last fall, the City of Charleston discovered that removal of statues of Lee and Stonewall Jackson would cost $700,000 – taxpayer dollars. No word yet on what removal will cost the Crescent City. On the other hand, no one seems yet to have calculated the cost with interest of the rental value of the land and maintenance costs over all those years.

CONSISTENCY – WHAT ABOUT ALL THE OTHERS?

As Emerson said, "A foolish consistency is the hobgoblin of little minds ..." Yet one of the principal arguments against removal of any monument is that, for example, if we remove monuments of all who owned slaves, for that reason, then we must remove all, including the statue of William Penn atop City Hall, and the names of Washington, Penn, Franklin, and Logan from our city squares, as they all owned slaves. Colonial intellectual David Rittenhouse is the only square honoree not so stained. He was, however, the first American to sight Uranus.

As my guitar-playing brother Scott, a New Orleans attorney, points out in a classic reductio ad absurdum argument, we might also have to change the title of the Lennon-McCartney classic, "Penny Lane," as that street was named after the 18th Century Liverpool slave ship captain, James Penny. "Very strange ..."

The New Orleans decision in the cases of the Lee, Davis, and Beauregard statues is readily defensible against the consistency criticism. Unlike the Philadelphia examples, this unseemly triumvirate were actually traitors who began and perpetuated a civil war. And, of course, a monument to a "battle" for 'white supremacy' is sui generis offensive.

BALANCE

As with any political decision in a democracy with many fundamental principles and beliefs that are often conflicting, we must weigh and balance all facts, principles, and goals. Before we erect or remove any public monument marker or similar honorific, we must conduct a deliberate, dispassionate, thorough, and thoughtful analysis of the person's entire life, the character, action or event at hand, and determine what positive we seek to convey and what negative perceptions might ensue. This is precisely what the Philadelphia Bar Foundation did when it considered removal (and ultimately did remove) of the name of "Andrew Hamilton" from its annual gala. (www.philadelphiabarfoundation.org/news/ad-hoc-committee-report)

MEN CAN CHANGE

Our own Benjamin Franklin is a good and difficult example of why a person's entire life must be examined. Yes, he owned a few household slaves for a while, but late in life, he had a change of heart, becoming president of the first American abolitionist organization, the Pennsylvania Anti-Slavery Society, which presented the first Petition for the Abolition of Slavery to the House of Representatives. To date, Ben has been spared removal talk.

LONGSTREET

Charles Lane of The Washington Post has advocated that the Lee statue should be replaced with one of the former Confederate General who led a bi-racial state militia against the white supremacists at the "Battle of Liberty Place" – James Longstreet. Although he fought for the Confederacy as part of Lee's inner circle, he accepted defeat and urged his former soldiers and their countrymen to support the Federal government and rebuild the South on principles of racial tolerance and equality. He died 39 years after the war, reviled by most Southerners as a traitor to The Lost Cause and, just as sadly, unheralded by any in the North for his change of heart and post-war good works.

OLD HICKORY

Like Franklin, Andrew Jackson presents a delicate dilemma. Take'em Down NOLA also wants the removal of the Clark Mills' equestrian statue of Jackson, erected in 1856, which stands in the center of the French Quarter's Jackson Square (Place D'Armes) on the riverfront before St. Louis Cathedral. Although the private Jackson Monument Association initiated the effort to erect the Jackson statute, the state contributed funds and the City the land. Though added in 1862 by Union General Benjamin Butler in a parting shot to unrepentant Rebels, the pedestal states, in succinct Jacksonian prose, "The Federal Union, It Must And Shall be Preserved." Identical Jackson statues stand in Nashville, Tenn. (1880), Jacksonville, Fla. (1987), and, in Washington, D.C. (1853), in Lafayette Park across from the White House.

Although a slave owner all his life (150 at his death in 1845) and the annihilator of the Creek Indian Nation, Jackson did defeat the British at the Battle of New Orleans, almost single handedly made populist politics our national religion, and saved the Union and prevented civil war in the 1832 – Nullification Crisis.

Old Hickory's New Orleans statue is unique in another way – it has become an iconic symbol of the Crescent City where the #1 industry is tourism ($7 billion a year). Thus, its value to the City is actually quantifiable and substantial. Not so with the replicas or The Four slated for the dustbin of history.

"LONG TIME COMING"

In the early morning damp darkness of April 24, 2017, masked, bullet-proof vested workers, guarded by dozens of police, including snipers, removed the first of The Four, the most offensive, "The Battle of Liberty Place" monument. In less than four hours, it was dismantled and gone. Finally, as Al Dandridge, past Chancellor of the Philadelphia Bar Association, decried, "Long time coming."

The irony was palpable. The first public event in American history protected by government snipers was the First Inaugural of Abraham Lincoln. Both times, they served their purpose – to deter violent racists from disrupting democracy in action. Just for good measure, April 24th was "Confederate Memorial Day."

Communities throughout this nation will inevitably address such issues in time. After all, one day someone may erect a statute of our current president.

POSTSCRIPT:

"FROM LOGAN TO LINCOLN SQUARE"

In 2012 I discovered that the only spot where President Abraham Lincoln publicly spoke in Philadelphia was not marked in any way. I spearheaded an effort to erect an Historical Marker at the site on Logan Square and it now stands there.

Recently, while strolling past the Marker, I noticed a group of African-American school children standing around it while their teacher explained to them that the man who freed their ancestors from slavery had spoken at that spot.

A touching moment to be sure.

They probably did not also know that Lincoln spoke and they stood in a public square named in honor of another man who was a slave owner and slave trader, James Logan.

The irony was palpable.

As should be our public shame.

No city public square, least of all one of the five original ones should be named for a man who owned and traded other human beings.

Yes, three other of the five squares are also named for men who owned slaves –Washington, Franklin and Penn. However, while not forgetting or excusing those substantial blemishes on the characters of those men, their singular contributions to this nation's and this state's history merit certain honor.

Not so much with James Logan.

While also a man of impressive accomplishments, his pale in comparison to those of Washington, Franklin, Penn and even Rittenhouse (the only non-slave owner city square honoree).

Not only did Logan own and trade in slaves, but he was personally responsible for swindling the Lenni-Lenape (Delaware) Indians of 1.2 million acres of land in the infamous Walking Purchase of 1737.

And we honor this man today?

I doubt whether more than a handful of Philadelphians know who Logan was and an even smaller number know he was a slave owner/trader.

In 1825 when the City honored James Logan by naming North West Square after him, only 8% of the city was black. And over 300 were still slaves.

Today over 44% of the City is African-American and each such citizen must live with and pay to maintain a public space honoring a slave owner/trader.

That is just wrong.

Since Ferguson, the issue of race and the legacy of slavery has been at the forefront of public concern unlike any time since the 1960's. All across the country state and municipal governments have been reassessing the naming of public works after slave owners, traders, overseers and those who fought to maintain that wretched "Peculiar Institution."

The City of Philadelphia should change the name of Logan Square from that of a man who owned and sold slaves to that of the man who freed them.

Logan Square should become LINCOLN SQUARE.

The removal of the Logan honorific is particularly timely in light of the upcoming opening of the Museum of the American Revolution which will feature a replica of the statue of King George III toppled by Patriots in New York City on July 9, 1776.

Let us remind the world that as Lincoln said at Gettysburg, we really are that "nation, conceived in liberty, and dedicated to the proposition that all men are created equal" and "have a new birth of freedom."

"THE TIMES THEY ARE A CHANGIN'"[8]

Students of history often ponder "what ifs?" – what if one thing happened before another?, what if one decision had been made instead of another? One in particular fascinates and haunts – August 20, 1619, Jamestown, Virginia – the day African men, women and children first set foot on this continent as slaves offered for sale. 'What if?' one or a few leaders in that small, experimental colonial community had stood up and said, "No. Slavery is wrong and we will not have it here. Take these people back to their homes and set them free. Or be arrested and jailed here for your natural life by man and damned to hellfire for all eternity by a righteous God."

Unfortunately, no one so spoke and, as they say, the rest is history.

In the summer of 2015 while doing research for a column, the then Editor-in-Chief of this magazine, discovered that the man we have long revered as <u>the</u> "Philadelphia Lawyer," Andrew Hamilton had a dark secret – he had been a plantation overseer and a slave owner. Although our <u>TPL</u> colleague, Steve LaCheen, had previously exposed some of Hamilton's less than savory acts, including fraud, sexual abuse and abuse of public office ("A Fragment of Our Legal History: Andrew Hamilton Accused," <u>TPL</u>, Spring 2002), neither he nor anyone else in the Bar seemed to know of Hamilton's ownership of other human beings.

The fact was surprising, but even more so the fact of our collective ignorance of same combined with our virtual worship of this "one-hit wonder," as Steve called him. By the way, as it turns out, he probably does not deserve so much credit for even his "one hit" (the Zenger Trial victory) as it was conceived and authored by another. See the Book Review later in this issue.

---

[8] <u>The Philadelphia Lawyer</u>, Vol. 80, No. 3, Fall 2017, Co-Authored with Niki Ingram, Esq. and Al Dandridge, Esq.

In any event, realizing that the Philadelphia Bar Foundation's grand gala event and fundraiser was named for Andrew Hamilton, we knew that something had to be done. First, he was outed, so to speak, in an Editorial ("Sounds of Silence," TPL, Summer 2015). Second, before approaching the Bar Foundation Board, the issue was brought to the TPL Editorial Board which always ensures lively debate. The TPL Board agreed that we should bring this to the attention of the Bar Foundation Board and suggest that the gala name be changed to something more fitting its noble goals.

Bar Foundation President, Steven Bizar, was quite receptive to the information and the idea.

The Foundation formed an ad hoc committee to examine whether continuing to refer to its annual fundraising dinner as the Andrew Hamilton Benefit was the best way to further its mission of promoting equal access to justice or whether a new name that described the Foundation's mission would work better to advance its goals.

The ad hoc committee, of which Chancellor and now TPL Board Member, Al Dandridge was a member, was composed of local prominent attorneys, as well as several past chancellors of the Philadelphia Bar Association.

After extensive research, debate and deliberation, the committee, in a superbly crafted report, recommended to the Bar Foundation that Hamilton's name be removed from the fundraising event. (www.philadelphiabarfoundation.org/news/ad-hoc-committee-report)

The committee's deliberations were thoughtful, somber and heartfelt. Obviously no one condoned slavery. The question for the day was what should be done to resolve the issue at hand. What happened more than 250 years ago – happened. Keep the name, remove the name, or provide more information so people can make their own judgments. No quarrel would be made with any decision made in good faith and not sweeping the issue under the rug.

However, let us not speak for ourselves. Let us speak for a multitude of people in America who were of recent African descent at that time. Slavery was an institution that provided enormous wealth to the slave owners and a mechanism to ensure white supremacy. It was cruel, barbaric and inhumane. Africans did not choose this as their fate or the fate of their children or children's children. Clearly, the hypothetical ability to speak out at Jamestown, Virginia on August 20, 1619 was offered to the wrong group of people standing on that dock.

The removal of Andrew Hamilton's name from the Bar Foundation's Fundraising Ball is consistent with the values of the Philadelphia Bar Association, the Philadelphia Bar Foundation and the society in which we live. Over the last few years colleges and universities have apologized for their roles in slavery; cities and states have removed the statutes of confederate soldiers; and serious debates have occurred and continue to take place about how the legacy of public figures who were slaveholders. These conversations make us all stronger, as they make us realize that while much of life is textured, there are absolutes. Our collective consciousness has been raised by these conversations and the recognition that the "peculiar institution" of slavery continues to impact our country more than one hundred years after the Emancipation Proclamation.

We recognize that how we view the world has changed the way in which we discuss slavery. There is greater understanding that the vestiges of slavery remain with us and permeate our educational system, our housing system and the distribution of wealth. The question become what does that mean in the context of this discussion? Given this backdrop, as the Bar Foundation Gala moves forward what should it now be called? There have been some suggestions that it should be renamed for a person of color and/or someone who has worked to advanced human rights. Perhaps the name should simply reflect the event and be known as the Philadelphia Bar Foundation Gala or Ball. This allows the event to stand on its own and to reflect the realities of the times, no what the year, and the goals of inclusivity of this bar association, this city and the world in which this important event occurs.

DAVID LLOYD

Although slavery was legal in Pennsylvania for most of his lifetime, David Lloyd, (1656 – 1731) was the first Philadelphia Lawyer to publicly (and vociferously) oppose it. Admitted to the bar in 1686, he was only one of seven lawyers in Philadelphia in 1708. Turns out he was quite the gadfly, if not the "first American revolutionary lawyer." While he did legal work for William Penn in London, in Pennsylvania he turned on his former client leading "Lloyd's Rebellion" against the Proprietor's prerogatives in favor of colonists' rights.

David Lloyd was really the first "Philadelphia Lawyer" and he, not his contemporary Andrew Hamilton, should be remembered and honored as such.

II. PAST AS PROLOGUE

"A NATION BORN OF, BUILT ON AND SAVED BY COMPROMISE"[9]

Much has been written of late of the strict, unyielding adherence of political parties and candidates to various principles or positions. This modern political trend of ideological purity seems to have roots in early 1950s McCarthyism but came to maturity with Senator Barry Goldwater (R-AZ) in the early 1960s who famously roared, "I would remind you that extremism in the defense of liberty is no vice."

That worked out so well for him.

The recent revival of purity of political principle has almost rendered "compromise" a four-letter word. But anyone with knowledge of and a sense of U.S. history understands that this nation was born of, built on and saved by compromises of many highly principled, but also pragmatic men. Unfortunately, so many of our politicians of today have little sense of our yesterday and those that do often selfishly misstate or misuse it.

The Oxford English Dictionary (2nd Ed., Clarendon Press, Oxford, Volume III, Page 636, Def. 4a) defines "compromise" as: "a coming to terms, or arrangement of a dispute, by concessions on both sides; partial surrender of one's position, for the sake of coming to terms." Like a good settlement in a lawsuit, in a good compromise neither party is really happy, but neither is really unhappy. Neither feels that he gave too much or got too little. This is not to say that one should readily or ever compromise on fundamental principles. The rub seems to be just what principles are "fundamental."

It is fitting that Philadelphia lawyers ruminate over this issue since this nation was founded and our Constitution was

---

[9] The Philadelphia Lawyer, Vol. 76, No. 2, Summer 2013

created here in a veritable cauldron of compromise in the stifling summers respectively of 1776 and 1787.

IN THE BEGINNING...

In that auspicious summer of 1776, the Second Continental Congress, 56 men (24 of them lawyers) met to decide how to respond to the 27 specific "repeated injuries and usurpations" of King George III so meticulously recounted by Thomas Jefferson in the Declaration of Independence. Jefferson's first draft was altered in several important respects, reflecting compromises amongst the five committee members designated to draft it, as well as Adams, Franklin and the entire Congress. The most significant change made by Congress was the complete removal of a stinging indictment of George III, holding him responsible for the slave trade, and indeed slavery itself, and for stimulating slave insurrection. Incongruously, the author, Jefferson, at the time owned 175 slaves. Southern delegates steadfastly refused to sign anything which questioned their "peculiar institution" and the others knew the entire enterprise would fail without unanimity, thus, they compromised. Curiously, while sheepishly protecting the right to enslave others, Congress, unlike Jefferson, insisted that the document include reference to the importance of God guiding their endeavor.

The Constitutional Convention of 1787 which produced the astounding framework of our government enduring these 224 years was successful precisely because those Framers were principled and practical. In fact, what has come down to us in history as The Great Compromise of 1787 (or "Connecticut" or "Sherman" Compromise) was the lynchpin which held the large and small states together in this then seemingly unlikely union. Roger Sherman's unoriginal though untried plan for proportional representation in the House and equal representation in the Senate was sufficiently attractive to states as disparate in size and population as Delaware and New York or Rhode Island and Virginia to bind all in union.

The Constitution was actually our fourth attempt to develop a structure to govern the "United Colonies/States" together.

The first, the Articles of Association in 1774, led to the Declaration of Independence in 1776, then to the Articles of Confederation of 1778, then to the Constitution of 1787, all born of compromises, large and small. Monarchs and tyrants have neither desire nor need to compromise. But elected representatives of the people should have the former and require the latter.

"The Great" was not the only compromise which enabled the 13 states to agree to a new form of government. At least four additional substantial compromises were required to ensure success of this difficult and noble endeavor -- The 3/5's Compromise, The Slave Trade Compromise, The Commerce Compromise and The Executive Election Comprise.

Not surprisingly, the festering sore of slavery required delicate attention lest the Southern states bolt and defeat the very purpose – "to form a more perfect union." Though no slave had a say in it, the Northern States held their noses and acquiesced in the counting of every five slaves as three persons for purposes of proportional representation. (Article I, Section 2)

Northerners also allowed tariffs only on imports rather than also on exports in order to mollify the heavily exporting South. (Article I, Section 8) Although accepting this federal commerce power then, over 30 years later, the South, via South Carolina, sought to nullify the Tariff of 1828, leading to a uniquely Jacksonian compromise, of which more later.

While Northerners wanted to end the slave trade immediately, they compromised - allowing Congress to do so only 20 years hence. (Article I, Section 9)

And lastly, some fearing that popular election of the President might not produce the best results, the Framers created a system of "electors" to act as a buffer to control the temperamental will of the people. In retrospect, it was probably the one real failed compromise of the famous five, or at least the one that has never really worked as originally intended. (Article II, Section 1)

COMPROMISES OF 1820, 1833, 1850 and 1877

From The Compromise of 1820 (Missouri Compromise) to the Compromise of 1877, our political leaders strove to hold the nation together, expand it and yet also deal with the thorny issue of slavery and its aftermath. Henry Clay (Whig/R-KY), said to be the most qualified man never to be president, bears the historical and honored moniker of "The Great Compromiser" for his pivotal role in bringing forth The Compromises of 1820 and 1850, as well as the Tariff Compromise during The Nullification Crisis of 1832-33.

Though a slaveholder himself, Clay lead the successful effort in 1820 to avoid civil war by his then ingenious plan, the Missouri Compromise, to admit Missouri as a slave state and Maine as a free state, thus maintaining the balance of 'slave versus free' in the Senate.

Again in 1833, Clay led the successful effort to reduce the Tariff of 1828 and to secure South Carolina's rescission of its "nullification" thereof. Though, truth be told, Jackson's threat to hang any man who refused to obey the federal law was at least equally as persuasive as the compromise reduction.

Clay's series of resolutions, now known as The Compromise of 1850, again averted civil war by maintaining a balance of interests between slave and free states.

And the last great event, which has merited the historical name "Compromise", with a capital "C", was the election/selection of Rutherford B. Hayes (R-Ohio) over Samuel J. Tilden (D-NY) in the 1876 Presidential race. Long before hanging chads and butterfly ballots of the Gore-Bush debacle of 2000, electoral disputes in four states, including Florida, put the victor unclear. Tilden won 51% of the popular vote, but the Electoral College was in disarray. After a bitter political and legal battle, an extra-legal, but eminently practical compromise was engineered in which Democrats accepted Hayes' "election" in exchange for Republican agreement to withdraw federal troops from the South.

Thus, this compromise, along with subsequent Supreme Court decisions, such as U.S. v. Cruikshank, 92 U.S. 5421 (1875) and The Civil Rights Cases, 109 U.S. 3 (1883), virtually abandoned the Negro in the South to the KKK and Jim Crow for the next century.

LESSONS FROM THE LEGAL PROFESSION

Like our judicial system, our legislative system simply cannot operate without compromise. Just as the absence of compromise would cause our courts to grind to an embarrassing halt, so would same lead our lawmaking apparatus to gridlock. While some may invite that doomsday scenario, it is as unwise as it is impractical.

Recent studies indicate that less than two percent of federal civil cases actually go to trial. A study in 2008 by Decision Set showed that for those uncompromising parties who chose to not settle and go to trial, only 15% were "right" to go to trial in that they did better at trial than they did in proffered pre-trial compromises. Thus, empirical evidence supports common sense. Compromise works. Intransigence is unwise.

Is there something that we who toil in the bowels of the judicial system can teach our friends and representatives in the legislative branch? Have we not all heard the bluster of opposing counsel at the outset of a case that his client will not accept anything but all that is requested in the Complaint or, if defending, dismissal with prejudice and payment of his legal fees and costs? I have. Hundreds of times, but seldom, in 34 years of practice, have I seen any case end that way for either side.

Anyone who has clerked for or served on an appellate court, if candid, will tell you that there is compromise aplenty in chambers, if not on holdings, certainly on the language chosen to support and explain same. And let us not forget that we go out of our way to encourage compromise by cloaking such discussions/offers with the protection of inadmissibility.

And any good mediator knows, creative lawyers are most apt to settle a case and do so more quickly. Even the intransigent and uncompromising can often be brought around by an innovative solution. Such as it was that Alexander Hamilton solved the otherwise apparently insurmountable problem of states' revolutionary war debts in 1790 and Sherman solved the large versus small state dilemma in 1787.

GRADUALISM

The Darwinian concept of gradualism, the hand maiden of compromise, also has deep roots in our history. That profound change can often best be brought about in small, incremental ways, rather than abrupt strokes is well supported in our history. In fact, the most despicable aspect of the most intractable problem of our first 100 years, the slave trade, was deftly handled in the Constitution via compromise and gradualism. Rather than end this insidious human commerce by fiat, the Framers permitted it to die a slow, but certain death 20 years hence, albeit it in cryptic fashion, without even mentioning any form of the word slave (Article I, Section 9). On the first day permitted by the Constitution, Congress outlawed the slave trade and the nation survived for another 52 years without civil war. This is perhaps the prime example in our history of successful compromise and gradualism, but it was shortly followed with another, courtesy of the creativity of the bastard of Nevis.

A CAPITAL FOR DEBT RELIEF

Alexander Hamilton engineered Compromise of 1790 at the famous Maiden Lane dinner with Jefferson and Madison in New York which ensured that the federal government would assume the revolutionary war debts of all states, a point incredibly important to Northern states in particular, and, in exchange, that the capital of the new nation would be built in the South, but would move to and be in Philadelphia for 10 years until it was built — classic compromise and gradualism.

EVEN THE MIGHTY

One might think that leaders such as Jackson, Lincoln or Kennedy never compromised. But they all did. Jackson threatened to hang the leaders of the Nullification Crisis of 1833, but he agreed to lower the tariff rather than have to do so. Lincoln repeatedly said that he would do almost anything to keep the Union together and he often did. He proposed plans for compensated emancipation, gradual emancipation and even ill-conceived and ill-fated colonization, but to no avail. And Kennedy, as any modern president must, often compromised, including when on the brink of nuclear war in 1962. Although he sheepishly hid the details from the people, Kennedy compromised substantially with Khrushchev agreeing not to invade Cuba (again) and to remove our Jupiter short-range nuclear missiles from Turkey.

FAILURE TO COMPROMISE

While our history abounds with failures to compromise and opportunities lost, three in particular deserve special mention.

Every modern politician knows and follows the unwritten rule that no member of Congress can vote against supplying troops in the field, no matter how much he opposes the cause, but few know that this is the direct result of the bitter lesson learned by the Federalists during the War of 1812. Refusing to compromise their principled opposition to that war, Federalist members of Congress repeatedly voted against supplies for the troops in the field and that party was rapidly relegated to the dustbin of history as a direct result.

After compromising for over 80 years, Southern politicians failed to compromise again in 1860 and paid a heavy price for their intransigence. One is reminded of the heady arrogance of the Tarleton boys, Charles Hamilton and other Southern gentlemen at the antebellum Twelve Oaks picnic in "Gone With The Wind." That worked out so well for them.

Lastly, Woodrow Wilson and Senator Henry Cabot Lodge failed to compromise on ratification of the Treaty of Versailles, in particular the infamous Article X which would have authorized the League of Nations to go to war without Congressional approval. The result was an international organization without the U.S. utterly incapable of stopping Mussolini, Hitler, Stalin or anyone else.

THUS ENDETH THE LESSON

Whether it is in our most intimate, personal relationships or the great affairs of state, willingness to compromise is a time-honored, enduring and noble characteristic that has always and will always continue to make us a better people and a better nation.

Let us hope that our political parties, candidates and office holders heed the 1905 warning of philosopher George Santayana, that "Those who cannot remember the past are condemned to repeat it."

"HOW LAWYERS WON (AND LOST) THE CIVIL WAR"

I am often asked by those planning to visit Philadelphia for the first time what they must see here. Without hesitation, I say, The National Constitution Center. Invariably, I then have the difficult task of explaining why a building dedicated to a 7-article, 8,000-word legal document written by a 55-member committee 226 years ago should be of interest to any other than attorneys and history buffs.

I have the same difficulty when I try to explain why and how this nation, only 150 years ago, fought its most terrible war to ensure the sanctity of that very legal document. Yes, our Civil War was fought to preserve the Union created on June 21, 1788, the day that New Hampshire, the ninth state, ratified the Constitution that had been completed here in The Pennsylvania State House on September 17, 1787.

Indeed, that internecine conflict, in which more died than in all of our other wars combined, was not only based upon the preservation of a legal principle, but also, arguably, won by our society's protectors of such principles, its lawyers, including some Philadelphia lawyers.

While there can be no doubt that the military victories of West Point-trained engineers Grant, Sherman (also a lawyer), Meade and others brought the rebel forces to their knees, it was the political leadership and legal maneuvers of many trained and experienced in our profession which enabled those victories, preserved the Union and brought the war to what was not its inevitable conclusion.

All know that Abraham Lincoln was a successful trial lawyer for almost a quarter of a century before he ascended to the presidency and that during the war he drafted and issued perhaps the most famous legal document authored by one man – The Emancipation Proclamation. What many may not know is that lawyers filled the leadership of his cabinet, his administration, the Army, the Navy and the Congress, and collectively, they created, defended and protected a wide variety of legal principles which brought military victory, preservation of the Union and the end of slavery.

During his tenure as Chief Magistrate Lincoln would appoint hundreds of lawyers to a wide variety of civilian and military positions, beginning with his second hire – newly minted young lawyer, John Hay, as his junior secretary.

Lincoln's first vice president, Hannibal Hamlin was a lawyer, as were eleven of the thirteen men who served in his Cabinet, his "Team of Rivals": Edwin M. Stanton, Secretary of War (second); William H. Seward, Secretary of State; Salmon P. Chase, (first), William Pitt Fessenden, (second) and Hugh McCulloch (third), Secretaries of Treasury; Edward Bates (first) and James Speed (second), Attorneys General; Caleb Blood Smith, (first) and John Palmer Usher (second) Secretaries of the Interior; Montgomery Blair (first) and William Dennison, Jr., (second), Postmasters General. Only Lincoln's first Secretary of War, lackluster Pennsylvania politician Simon Cameron and Secretary of the Navy, Connecticut newspaper publisher Gideon Welles, were not members of the bar. Welles, however, whom Lincoln affectionately called "Neptune," actually had a legal education but was never admitted to the bar.

Peter H. Watson, a Washington patent attorney, served under Stanton as Assistant Secretary of War, and on more than one occasion was designated by Lincoln as Acting Secretary of War. Seward was so close to Lincoln that it was often said that he was in effect, Lincoln's "prime minister." The influence of Stanton and Chase was only marginally less so. And this in an era, unlike the present, when presidents actually met regularly with, relied heavily on and consulted often with their Cabinet members.

While Stanton deserves much praise for the Union's military victory, Chase and Welles are two particularly unsung lawyer heroes of the war. Chase masterfully managed the nation's finances enabling the federals to field overwhelming manpower and material, in part by innovative legislation, including the first Income

Tax (Internal Revenue Act - 1861), a new National Bank (National Bank Act – 1863) and the first national currency, "greenbacks" (Legal Tender Act – 1862). His financial wizardry stood in stark contrast to the disastrous bumbling of Confederate Secretary of The Treasury, non-lawyer Christopher Memminger. Secretary Welles took a pitiful 42-ship wooden U.S. Navy and turned it into one of the most modern and powerful ironclad maritime military forces that had ever existed, in less than three years, seizing New Orleans, opening the Mississippi and choking Southern ports.

Lincoln also relied on lawyers to keep Britain and France from recognizing and supplying the Confederacy. His key ministers to Great Britain, Charles Francis Adams, and to France, William L. Dayton, were lawyers. So, too, was his minister to Mexico, Thomas Corwin who helped prevent supplies from pouring into the Confederacy through our neighbor to the South.

Even in times of grief, Lincoln was with members of our profession when his favorite son, Willie, died on February 20, 1862, he was consoled by Reverend Francis Vinton of New York City's Trinity Church – also a lawyer.

LAWYERS ALSO LOST – CSA, ESQ.

As there are always two sides to an argument, there are most often lawyers on both sides. And that is as it should be. And as it was in 1860. In fact, lawyers led the secession debacle – 42 of the 59 members of the Provisional Confederate Congress were lawyers.

Not coincidentally, the Confederate military forces were led by many lawyers, including Generals Jubal A. Early, Maxcy Gregg, John G. Gordon, Samuel Garland, Roberdeau Chatham Wheat, Joseph Brevard Kershaw, William Tatum Wofford, Ambrose Ransom Wright, John Singleton Mosby, Edwin H. Stoughton, Basil Duke, Charles Minor Blackford, Thomas Goode Jones, Albert Pike and Admiral Raphael Semmes.

While Mosby, Early and Semmes had some spectacular victories over Union forces, in the end, neither theirs, nor the efforts of their co-counsel generals were sufficient to best the legal juggernaut of the Union counselors.

Confederate President Jefferson Davis was not a lawyer, but his older brother and mentor, Joseph was. As was his Vice President, Alexander H. Stephens, and all but two of his cabinet members. The irascible Davis went through five Secretaries of War – all lawyers, and all failed him. Although Lincoln had similar troubles with his first Secretary of War, and with trying to find a General In Chief who would fight and win, he eventually found Stanton and Grant. And victory.

GREAT GRANDFATHER'S JAILER

Union Major General John Alexander McClernand, Springfield, Illinois, lawyer and friend and sometime political ally of Lincoln, led a force of 33,000 Federals against 5,500 Confederates on Jan. 11, 1863 (10 days after The Emancipation Proclamation) capturing Fort Hindman, and virtually all of its defending rebel soldiers, including my great grandfather, at The Battle of Arkansas Post. Private Milton Jared Tillery (farmer, not a lawyer) was released in a prisoner's exchange at City Point, Va., on April 12, 1863, not long before Grant, fed up with his insubordinance, cashiered the private's jailer, McClernand. This "political" general returned to the law, became a judge after the war and is buried not far from Lincoln in Oak Ridge Cemetery in Springfield.

PRESIDENTS

Twelve of our first sixteen presidents were lawyers. Though none had particularly impressive military exploits in the war, five who would later be president served the Union cause, all lawyers – Rutherford B. Hayes, James A. Garfield, Chester A. Arthur, Benjamin Harrison and William McKinley, though he was only admitted to the bar after the war.

Future President Grover Cleveland, also a lawyer, when drafted, avoided service by hiring Polish immigrant, George Benninsky, for $150 as a substitute in accord with The Enrollment Act.

PHILADELPHIA LAWYERS

Though the most prominent Philadelphians in the war, Union Generals George B. McClellan and George Gordon Meade were not lawyers, many Philadelphia lawyers contributed to the cause. The most effective, Horace Binney, did so not with sword, but with pen, writing three very persuasive pamphlets defending Lincoln's suspension of the Writ of Habeas Corpus. Lincoln and Grant both called upon him for counsel.

John Graver Johnson, destined to become the most prominent American corporate lawyer of The Gilded Age served proudly, if briefly and undistinguished, as a private in Battery A, First Pennsylvania Artillery, seeing some action around Gettysburg, not four months after being admitted to the bar. Charles E. Morgan, later founder of Morgan, Lewis & Bockius, served in Johnson's unit. Dozens of other prominent members of the Philadelphia Bar also served.

GENERAL WILLIAM TECUMSEH SHERMAN, ESQUIRE

Though he once disparaged our profession saying "I would rather be a blacksmith," William Tecumseh Sherman was a member of the Kansas Bar and practiced law there for a couple of years. His talents were, however, decidedly on the battlefield, not in the courtroom. He tried only two cases and lost both. However, his brilliant March to the Sea brought the reality of war to those who sent their sons to destroy the Union, leaving no doubt that, "War is Hell."

UNION GENERALS

While Sherman and McClernand stand out, the war was waged successfully by many other lawyers who took up the sword. When the war began, the small and widely dispersed U.S. Army (15,259 enlisted men; 1,105 officers – 296 resigned to join the CSA) was led by Lt. General Winfield Scott ("Old Fuss and Feathers"), a lawyer, who had entered the army in 1809, the year Lincoln was born. Scott authored the plan to encircle and choke the South by blockade – a plan that while harshly derided ("The Anaconda Plan") was ultimately quite effective.

Although other Union lawyer-generals made their marks, for good or otherwise, such as Henry Wager Halleck ("Old Brains"), Daniel Sickles, Lew Wallace, John A. Logan, John A. Dix, Edward S. Bragg, Nathaniel P. Banks, Carly Schurz, Thomas Ewing, Jr., Robert H. Milroy, Francis Channing Barlow, David Bell Birney, Thomas Francis Mergher, Daniel Butterfield, General Benjamin Franklin Butler deserves special mention.

While he may be best remembered as "Beast Butler" for his famous (or infamous) May 15, 1862 "Woman's Order" allowing any New Orleans woman who disrespected a Union Soldier to be "treated as a woman of the evening," he was a creative, clever lawyer with a sardonic sense of humor. His May 24, 1861 "Fort Monroe Declaration" that he could legally seize slaves as "contraband" property of the enemy led directly to the First and Second Confiscation Acts, then to the Emancipation Proclamation and, ultimately, to the 13th Amendment ending slavery.

Though lawyers are often disliked, Butler was so detested in the South that in December 1862 Jeff Davis issued an "Outlawing Proclamation" against him authorizing his immediate execution upon capture.

Philadelphian George Gordon Meade who led the Union triumph at Gettysburg was interested in the law as a young man, but his mother persuaded him to attend West Point. After the war in July 1865, he did receive an honorary Doctor of Laws degree from Harvard.

LINCOLN'S CODE

While its very name is an oxymoron, our "Civil" War gave us the world's first codification of the equally facially ironic "laws" of war. In early 1863, Secretary of War Stanton and General-in-Chief Henry Halleck, troubled by the absence of clear legal guidelines on how to deal with the rebels, charged Columbia Professor Francis Lieber, L.L.D., with drawing up a legal code to govern armies in battle. On April 24, 1863, the War Department, with Lincoln's imprimatur issued General Order No. 100 in 157 Articles – "Instructions For The Government of Armies of The United States In The Field." Though Lieber was its principal draftsman, it would come to be known as "Lincoln's Code," "a seminal document in the history of civilization" (historian and lawyer John Fabian Witt), and form the basis for the first and many subsequent Geneva Conventions.

Article 57-58 ("The law of nations know of no distinction of color, …") which prohibited discrimination against enemy soldiers on the basis of race stands out as the first Federal racial anti-discrimination legal measure. The irony that black prisoners of war might have more rights to equal treatment under law than free blacks even in the North was lost on most at the time. Just as was the more stark irony that had the U.S. not secured independence based on 'all men being created equal,' in 1776, American slaves would have been freed not in 1865, but 32 years earlier in 1833 when Great Britain freed all slaves in its colonies.

Though there were notable and tragic exceptions like the Fort Pillow Massacre and Andersonville, both armies generally followed the principles set forth in The Code and as a result, a long and awful war was made not longer and more awful.

JUDGE ADVOCATES

Lincoln had substantial legal talent supporting his efforts to maintain the Union in the courts and other legal forums. His Army Judge Advocate General, Joseph Holt, guided a team of thirty-three first-class lawyer Judge Advocates who rendered opinions upholding Lincoln's various legal war measures including seizure of property and slaves, Emancipation, suspension of the Writ of Habeas Corpus and use of Military Commissions. The last was of particular import as it enabled Lincoln to sidestep the unpredictability of state and federal judges and juries in almost 4,000 military proceedings bringing swift justice to a wide variety of miscreants who threatened the Union and the war effort.

LITANY OF LEGAL ISSUES

The war was, of course, begun based upon two fundamental legal disputes over The Constitution – whether slavery could be prohibited in new territories and states and whether a state could secede from the Union. On both, the Constitution is silent, or, at least, deliberately ambiguous. While reasonable lawyers of good faith could and did argue these points ad nauseam before and during the war, numerous other important legal issues arose and greatly impacted the outcome of the war. Virtually all of those issues concerned the legal status of persons and property.

Lincoln's first legal war measure concerned the status of persons arrested. On April 27, 1861, only five days after Major Robert Anderson surrendered the Federal garrison at Fort Sumter, Lincoln authorized General Scott to suspend the Writ of Habeas Corpus on the railroad lines from Philadelphia to Washington. Pursuant thereto, Philadelphia lawyer, General George Cadwalader arrested and held Maryland politician John Merryman and refused to obey such a writ, leading to Chief Justice Roger B. Taney's order to release him in Ex Parte Merryman (17 F.CAS. 144 (C.C.D. Md. 1861). Although Taney ruled Lincoln's act unconstitutional, the President ignored the Chief Justice and Congress later ratified and authorized his act that proved a powerful, and often used, war measure.

Lincoln's next such legal act concerned the status of shipping – the equally arguably illegal act of the blockade (not "port closure") of the Southern ports. While risking recognition by France and England of the Confederacy as a sovereign nation, if not war with those nations, Lincoln used this legal measure, reserved for time of war between sovereign nations, to effectively cut off the ill-equipped South from ready access to foreign arms and other support. Its legality was upheld in the Prize Cases, 67 U.S. 635 (1863).

And last, but certainly not least, were the many legal issues and acts concerning the status of the four million slaves in the Confederacy and Border States. As the Fugitive Slave Laws (based, by the way, on a Constitutional provision, Article IV, Section 2) fell into disuse and as Union generals from Fremont to Butler to Hunter welcomed runaway slaves into Union lines, Congress passed and Lincoln signed the First and later the Second Confiscation Acts authorizing Union officers to seize and use rebel property used in war-making, including slaves. Lincoln then issued the preliminary Emancipation Proclamation on September 22, 1862, and the final on January 1, 1863. And the 13th Amendment finally passed the House on February 4, 1865. Slavery died a slow, legal death, as the war drew to a close.

As Historian Richard Hofstadter observed, the Emancipation Proclamation "had all the moral grandeur of a Bill of Lading." Karl Marx said it was like "the trite summonses that one lawyer sends to an opposing lawyer, the legal chicaneries and pettifogging stipulations of an actiones juris." But what neither fully appreciated is that it was consciously intended to be a cold, dispassionate legal document so that it would withstand challenge in the courts. Lincoln, the author, and his cabinet member lawyers who vetted it made it so. Fortunately for Lincoln and the nation, the passage of the 13th Amendment (December 18, 1865) mooted any legal challenge to that momentous "scrivener's drivel."

Freeing the slaves in areas under rebellion helped deprive the Confederate military of much-needed manpower. Confederate armies were supported by thousands of slave laborers, (at least one slave for every two soldiers) many of whom melted away after January 1, 1863. That fact, together with the raising of black Union troops starting in May of that same year (almost 200,000 would serve), what Lincoln himself called "the heaviest blow yet," made defeat of the traitors inevitable.

FIVE LAWYERS ON A BOAT

Two months before Lee surrendered, on February 3, 1865, Lincoln and Seward met three Confederate "Peace Commissioners" on the River Queen steamboat at Hampton Roads, Va. near Fort Monroe. Confederate Vice President and old friend of Lincoln's, Alexander H. Stephens, CSA Senator Robert M.T. Hunter and CSA Assistant Secretary of War John A. Campbell were all lawyers. Arranged by a sixth lawyer, Francis Preston Blair, Sr., friend of both Lincoln and Davis, this "settlement conference" failed to bring peace as Lincoln made clear that Union was the precondition for peace and, by some accounts, that slavery was already effectively dead. The recalcitrant commissioners had no authority to agree to the demise of the Confederacy, so they forced a 'fiery trial' – by battle. As with most stubborn and doctrinaire litigants, it went rather badly for them.

'PRESENT AT THE TERMINATION'

The central players at the surrender of the Army of Northern Virginia on April 9, 1865 at Appomattox Courthouse were not lawyers, but Robert Todd Lincoln, the president's son, then a law student was there as one of General Grant's aides along with a young lawyer, John A. Rawlins, upon whom Grant often relied. Since there were then still other Confederate armies in the field, the war actually ended, arguably, when the Confederate Commander-in-Chief,

Jefferson Davis, was captured a month later on May 10, 1865 near Irwinville, Georgia, by the 4th Michigan Cavalry, led, perhaps not coincidentally by Lieutenant Colonel Benjamin D. Pritchard, a lawyer from Allegan, Michigan.

"PATENTLY CONFEDERATE"

The Founding Fathers endeavored four months in convention here in the sweltering summer of 1787 to debate and draft the Constitution. The ratification process consumed another nine months.

Three score and fourteen years later, the Founding Traitors of the Confederate States of America, in convention in Montgomery, Alabama, took only five days to form a Provisional Government, 26 more to draft, and 12 more to debate and self-ratify their Constitution.

While those southern gentlemen might have seemed more efficient or capable, remember that they used the U.S. Constitution as a convenient template, though infecting it with the seed of their own destruction – the "cornerstone" of their Confederacy – slavery.

Thousands of volumes have been written about our Constitution, how it was created, and how it has worked for these 228 years, but not so much exists about the Confederate Constitution. True, it was in place for only a tiny fraction of the time – four years, about 2% of ours. And for much of that time, in many parts of that "nation," it was inoperative or unenforceable.

But these men did create a new national government of legal institutions, laws, and courts to govern 12 million people, four million of whom legally were enslaved. And that government did actually operate for over four years, even though never recognized as such by this or any other nation.

As the son of a lawyer who was active in the local Civil War Round Table, I can remember in law school poring through volumes of "F.2d" and "F. Supp.," asking my father what happened to the court system in the Confederacy. He did not know, and in that pre-Internet era, the answers were not at our fingertips. I scoured his ample Civil War library and found little, as I did likewise at Penn's Biddle Law Library. Were there no Confederate Supreme Court Reporters? Or Confederate Reporters? Alas, my historical curiosity was soon overtaken by the need to understand the Rule in Shelley's Case.

That 40-year old inquiry resurfaced recently when I ran across a reference in some obscure footnote to Confederate patent law, which provided that if "the original inventor or discoverer of the art, machine or improvement for which a patent is solicited is a slave, the master of such slave … shall receive a patent for said discovery or invention." While it did not surprise me in the least that the C.S.A. had enacted yet another law to ensure that white men could legally steal the work of enslaved black men, who knew the Confederacy had a Patent Office?

Patents were only one of many legal issues with which the new Confederate government had to wrestle while preparing for war for its survival, but its handling of other such issues was quite similar. Only 12 days after its formation, the Provisional Government of the Confederate States of America, by signature of President Jefferson Davis, established a Patent Office in its also new Justice Department. New inventions, particularly those relating to weaponry, were very important to the secessionists, and they intended to give the Rhetts, Randolphs, and Ashleys of this new nation incentive to invent. The wording of the patent provision in the CSA Constitution was unchanged from that of the U.S. Constitution, and its patent law followed suit. Except for slave patent ownership, of course.

The Confederate Constitution provided for Confederate District Courts having, amongst other, exclusive jurisdiction over patent disputes. Thirteen such District Courts were established by the CSA Judiciary Act of 1861. There were provisions also for a Confederate Supreme Court, but none for intermediate courts of appeals. The Confederate Congress debated bills for the establishment of a Supreme Court for three years, but could never agree on its composition, jurisdiction, or powers. Thus, there was never a Confederate Supreme Court. The only Confederate courts were those District Courts which operated as courts of first and last resort for all patent, maritime, and other "confederate" issues.

There are no reporters collecting the cases of those District Courts, though the records of most Confederate District Courts do survive in the U.S. archives. (archives.gov) Nor have I found evidence that any cases involving Confederate patents were litigated during the few years in which these courts existed.

Not to be outdone by the United States in protecting its citizens' intellectual property, the Confederacy also provided for copyright protection in its Constitution and its Copyright Act of 1861, though the statute was virtually identical to the U.S. Copyright Act of 1831, then in effect. As with existing U.S. law, works to be copyrighted were filed not with any Copyright Office, as none existed, but with the author's local District Court Clerk. Likewise, no Confederate copyright cases seem to have made it to the courts.

Both Confederate patent and copyright law rather optimistically provided for registrants to have reciprocal protection with other nations that recognized the Confederacy. None ever did, unless you count the 15 Indian "nations," with which the CSA had treaties. None of them had any patent or copyright regimes.

As with almost every CSA official government position, the top job in the Patent Office was held by a man who had held and resigned a similar job with the Federal Government. In this case, Rufus Randolph Rhodes (even Margaret Mitchell could not make that one up) of Mississippi resigned his positions with the U.S. Patent Office as Patent Examiner and Member of the Board of Patent Appeals, and became CSA Chief Patent Clerk in July 1861.

Rhodes issued C.S.A. Patent Number 1 on August 1, 1861. 274 more would follow. The last was for a "pile driver" issued on March 21, 1865, just as Grant was closing in on Richmond. Some Patent Office records were loaded on the same last train out of Richmond on April 2, 1865 carrying the first, last, and soon to be captured President of the Confederate States of America. The CSA Patent Office itself, located with the War Department in the Mechanics Institute Building, burned to the ground later that night when Confederate soldiers torched nearby warehouses. Few records survived.

We do know that 275 Confederate patents issued. During the same period, 16,051 U.S. Patents issued. As with almost everything but bluster, the North had more resources and creativity. The bulk of Confederate patents were for weapons or other war-related products and agricultural machinery.

The most famous Confederate patent was Number 100, issued to John Mercer Brooke for the design of an ironclad ship which would be famously embodied in the C.S.S. Virginia, built on the burned out hull of the wooden C.S.S. Merrimack. Brooke's CSA patent was the subject of controversy during and long after the war, as it was based on original formal drawings and construction supervision of naval constructor John L. Porter. But Porter neither contested inventorship on the Patent Application in the Patent Office nor the Patent in court after it issued. Their dispute played out only in the newspapers.

Federal engineer and prolific inventor John Ericsson's U.S.S. Monitor, despite employing over 40 patented (U.S.) inventions, could fight Brooke's C.S.S. Virginia only to an inconclusive yet famous standoff at Hampton Roads, Virginia on March 9, 1862.

On May 8, 1862, Lincoln (the only President to be issued a Patent), his Secretary of State William H. Seward, and his Secretary of the Treasury Salmon P. Chase, aboard the revenue cutter U.S.S. Miami, almost got to witness a rematch. The "single patent" C.S.S. Virginia steamed into their view around Sewell's Point near Norfolk, Virginia, but hastily retreated when the "40 patent" U.S.S. Monitor and the U.S.S. Stevens, an ironclad battery, moved up to challenge her. Three days later, the Rebels blew up and torched the Virginia and the Monitor sailed up the James River toward Richmond.

In their prior professional lives as trial lawyers, Lincoln, Chase, and Seward had all handled significant patent cases.

Lincoln's then absent Secretary of War, Edwin M. Stanton, was also a very accomplished patent litigator.

The last time such an august assemblage had made an excursion on a U.S. warship, it did not end so well. In 1843 <u>Monitor</u> inventor Ericcson's then highly innovative screw propeller, among other features, made the <u>U.S.S. Princeton</u> (built in the Philadelphia Naval Yard) the most advanced warship of its time. Unfortunately, on a demonstration cruise on the Potomac on February 28, 1844, with President John Tyler and other dignitaries aboard, its 12- inch gun (<u>not</u> designed by Ericcson) "The Peacemaker" ruptured at the breech, instantly killing Secretary of State Abel P. Upshur, Secretary of the Navy Thomas Walker Gilmer, and six others, including two lawyers, Virgil Maxcy (MD.) and David Gardiner (N.Y.), and the President's valet, a slave known only as Armistead.

Rhodes estimated that at least 3,000 citizens of the Confederacy owned U.S. Patents, though, of course trying to enforce them or licenses on them in U.S. District Courts would have been problematic. Thus, at least for the duration of the war, these U.S. Patents had little value and could effectively be infringed at will in the U.S.

Likewise, U.S. citizens could not secure CSA patents, nor enforce U.S. patents in Confederate District Courts. But Confederate citizens could enforce their U.S. patents in Confederate District Courts, if they also registered them with the CSA Patent Office.

After the war, Confederate patents, like Confederate money, were worthless. However, in October 1866, citizens were permitted to apply for U.S. patents based on Confederate patents, and at least 25 Confederate patent holders did obtain U.S. patents on their Confederate inventions.

"NED'S" LAW

Confederate law stole from slave inventors, but U.S. law offered them no protection. In 1857, U.S. Commissioner of Patents (and Lincoln friend and confidante), Joseph Holt announced that slaves could not be granted patents because they were not "legally competent" to take the statutorily required oath. Former Pennsylvania Supreme Court Justice, Attorney General Jeremiah Sullivan Black (really!) had shortly before ruled that a slave master, Oscar J.E. Stuart, could not be issued a patent for an invention by his slave, "Ned," because Stuart was not the actual inventor. And "Ned" (last name unknown, if any) could not be issued a patent, either, because he was not a citizen of any country and as such could not take the required oath. Yet another example of legal "niceties" used to prevent the black man from enjoying the fruits of his own labor. It was not only the Confederates who did this in so many legally "creative" ways.

After the war, Rufus R. Rhodes, C.S.A. Commissioner of Patents, ardent supporter of slavery, secession, and patents, established a successful patent law practice in my hometown of New Orleans, expiring at the young age of 52 in 1870, just as Reconstruction was failing so miserably.

The secessionist, slave government was created, operated, and dissolved in just over four years. It, like its patents and patent regime, was quite properly, through at great cost of blood and treasure, relegated to the dustbin of history.

"AFFIRMATIVELY WHITE"

In preparation for a presentation at a Temple University Underground Railroad and Black History Conference on why Reconstruction failed, I re-read Ira Katznelson's 2005 seminal, yet overlooked work, <u>When Affirmative Action Was White – An Untold History of Racial Inequality in Twentieth Century America</u> and Ta-Neshi Coates' fascinating, yet controversial 2014 <u>Atlantic</u> article, "The Case For Reparations." Both expose government programs from 1932 on, which benefited primarily, if not often solely, white Americans, but neither address the issue from a longer historical perspective, that is, from the founding of the nation. Unfortunately, under government programs pre-New Deal, black Americans fared no better.

Needless to say, neither British nor colonial governments did much of anything to specifically benefit black Americans in the 155 years before Independence. True, Lord Dunmore did in 1775, as a war measure, offer freedom to any slave who would fight for the British. But every single domestic federal government program from July 4, 1776, until The Emancipation Proclamation on January 1, 1863 (also a war measure), was designed to and did benefit <u>only</u> white Americans. Four score and seven years of pure, lily white affirmative action.

The Act Prohibiting Importation of Slaves (March 2, 1807) ending the slave trade in 1808 certainly benefited only blacks. But African, <u>not</u> American.

Almost 500,000 of the 4.5 million black Americans were "free" before the 13th Amendment (Dec. 6, 1865), yet for them there was hardly an "even playing field" with white Americans. After April 1865, their numbers included 143,000 black Union veterans and their families and the families of 37,000 black men who gave their lives for the Union. Not only did black Americans <u>not</u> benefit from the largesse of a wide variety of federal government programs as whites did, but also they were actually affirmatively handicapped from advancing economically, educationally and politically, by a plethora of federal and state laws designed to do just that. Before and after the war.

On the morning of December 7, 1865, the sun rose, for the first time over a free America. Without slavery. Four million black human beings were suddenly, legally, undoubtedly, finally and forever free.

Yet, "free" without assets, education, land, homes, jobs, tools, farm implements, savings, credit, right to vote, witness in court, sit on a jury, hold elective office, or almost any other civil right, and most, without a last name.

Without any of those, the four million were expected to and had to compete in post-Civil War America with 27 million white Americans who had had those benefits and rights since the beginning of the Republic. An 89 year government-sponsored head start.

Further, most lived amongst six million Southern whites who did not want them there, did not want them to have any of those rights and benefits and were committed to using every possible legal and extra-legal means to stop any such acquisition.

On July 8, 1868, the 14th Amendment, in theory, guaranteed them citizenship, the privileges and immunities of same, the right to life, liberty and property not to be taken without due process, and equal protection of the law. Then on February 3, 1870, the 15th Amendment guaranteed them the right to vote.

To the 400,000 slave owners, the 13th Amendment might just as well have freed their livestock. For that is how they (and the law) viewed and treated the four million human beings they owned.

All of a sudden, it was if their cattle stood up and announced, "We are citizens, we will vote, we will be paid for our work and we will have equality. And, by the way, from now on we would like to be known as 'Bovine-Americans.'"

On that day, for the first time, all black Americans could, at least in legal theory, enjoy the fruits of their own labor, maintain the integrity of their families, marry and adopt, travel without a pass, own guns and dogs, drink/buy liquor, refuse to yield sidewalks to whites, dress as they pleased, educate themselves and their children, organize groups – churches, social, political, speak up in public, transfer assets at death, permit women to work only in the home, avoid sexual exploitation, own land and tools, save and borrow, sue, witness in court, serve on a jury, vote, run for/hold elected office, and have an inviolable home/person.

However, those and all legal rights are and were meaningless without effective remedies. And the federal and state legal system provided black Americans few, if any, remedies. None could afford lawyers. Although there were 33,193 lawyers in the U.S. in 1860, only 7 black lawyers had been admitted to any bar by 1865. Not even the most Radical Republican dreamt of Gideon, much less Civil Gideon. And redress of grievances from law enforcement (read – "white") was, unsurprisingly, virtually nonexistent.

By almost any measure, government programs and actions post-Civil War, even if facially neutral and/or unintended, benefited primarily white Americans at least until the mid-1960's.

Let us consider just a few. Black Americans were not U.S. or even State citizens until July 9, 1868 when the 14th Amendment was ratified. In fact, up until that point, the 1790 Naturalization Act specifically limited citizenship by naturalization to "free white persons" and it took Attorney General Edward Bates' 1862 Opinion to "clarify" that "free" black Americans born in the U.S. are actually citizens of the nation. Citizenship was not just an honorific, it was a requirement to vote, hold elective office, serve on juries and even own property in some states.

Civil War veterans and their dependents reaped a great bounty in government pensions. By 1900, over one million were still receiving benefits which accounted for over 22% of the Federal Budget. But, as with many federal benefits, though color-blind in legal entitlement, in reality, recent scholarship has shown that for a variety of reasons, few black veterans and their families received such benefits due.

Likewise, the cornucopia of wartime government contracts required to preserve the Union was given to white Americans whose taxpayer - created dynasties are household names today – Rockefeller, Swift, Armour, Morgan, Stanford, Pillsbury, Remington, etc.

After freedom, black Americans craved land more than anything. In all Southern states and many Northern states, however, they could not legally own land prior to 1868.

Between 1850 and 1871, under the Pacific Railway Acts of 1862 and 1864 and others, the Federal Government gave away over 1.31 million acres of public land and $64 million to railroads, owned and run only by white Americans.

The Mining Acts of 1866 and 1872 opened up millions of acres of public lands and thus vast, rich mineral resources to those capable of exploiting same – again, primarily white Americans.

The 1830 Indian Removal Act managed simultaneously to help white settlers while harming two non-white groups. It displaced several entire Indian tribes while redistributing their land to white settlers. And in 1870, the Federal Government terminated the Indian Treaty system which had treated tribes as nations, a move which benefited only white settlers, again.

The 1862 Homestead Act distributed 270 million acres of public lands overwhelmingly to white settlers. While the Southern Homestead Act of 1866 was, in part, intended to benefit black Americans by opening up another 46 million acres of government-owned Southern lands, only about 1,000 claims of black Americans were honored out of 27,800 grants.

While some land was distributed to a few Freedmen by the Freedmen's Bureau, General Sherman, Special Field Order No. 15 and others, virtually all of it was soon returned to its former owners - white Americans (former traitors), by the Federal Government, at the specific order of President Andrew Johnson.

Having been denied the right to learn to read and write for 246 years, Freedmen could not wait to educate themselves and, more importantly, their children. While the Freedmen's Bureau established thousands of schools throughout the South, they were, of course, segregated, underfunded and eventually most closed or were absorbed into white-dominated systems.

The Morrill Act of 1862 provided land and funding that created many land grant colleges, but none for black Americans until 1890. And then, until 1956, still all subject to the legal handicap of Plessy's "separate but equal." To be fair, 25 black colleges and universities, including Howard, Fisk, and Dillard, were established through the Bureau and are perhaps its great, enduring success and legacy.

Some say black Americans had the opportunity to share in all of this government largesse by electing over 1,500 federal and state office holders in the post-Civil War era. Putting aside the advent of the KKK, the Great Depression of the 1870's, Redeemer state governments, and Jim Crow laws, most of those offices were local and state and all black office holders were gone by 1900. In our entire history, only nine black Americans have served the U.S. Senate and only 131 black Americans have served in the U.S. House of Representatives. Two have served on the Supreme Court. One President.

Some argue that the Bureau of Refugees, Abandoned Lands and Refugees (Freedman's Bureau) transformed post-war American giving Freedmen astounding opportunities. Even this agency was not solely for black Americans by name or mandate and it did actually benefit many white (Southern) Americans. It had a noble and ambitious mandate, but it also had the first and largest unfunded mandate in our history. The Freedman's Bureau was unceremoniously terminated less than seven years after it was created. It did noble work, but at its peak, it only had 900 agents and expended only a total $18 million for four million people in 11 states - $4.50 per black American. In the slave market before 1865 each one was "worth" 100 times that. Even in today's dollars that $4.50 would only be about $64.00. Some affirmative action.

The demise of the Freedman's Bureau (1872), the end of Reconstruction and the withdrawal of Union troops from the South (1877), Jim Crow, the KKK and depression returned power in the South to the same social/political class that had seceded to protect and expand slavery, leaving most black Americans with no federal government benefits, much less protection, until the 1930's.

FDR's New Deal was, in theory, "a rising tide that lifted all boats," but Southern legislators forced a wide variety of compromises which ensured that these new government benefits would not flow to non-whites. The 1935 Social Security Act was a revolutionary measure, but it excluded agricultural and domestic workers, who not coincidentally, were primarily black Americans. Over 65% of all black Americans were ineligible.

That same year the National Labor Relations Act extended federal protection to collective bargaining, but permitted racial discrimination in unions which excluded black Americans from membership, an important stepping stone to the middle class well into the 1970's.

The National Housing Act of 1934 created the Federal Housing Administration which provided millions of white Americans with the opportunity to own a home, another key path to the middle class. Provisions for local administration resulting in "redlining" ensured that black Americans received few of these benefits until the late 1970's.

It is true, however, that many bills were introduced specifically to benefit black Americans. Most, including Anti-Lynching Acts in 1921, 1934 and 1940, suffered ignominious defeat. If Congress could not bring itself, 75 years after Appomattox, to protect black American lives against lawless hangings, legislation to protect their liberty, property or pursuit of happiness seemed unlikely.

The multi-billion dollar bonanza for corporate American brought by WWII went overwhelmingly to white Americans. Two-thirds of all government contracts went to just 100 corporations, all owned and controlled by white Americans.

FDR's Servicemen's Readjustment Act of 1944 a/k/a the G.I. Bill assisted millions of WWII veterans and their families with low-cost mortgages, low-interest loans to start businesses, grants for tuition and living expenses, unemployment benefits and other economic support. More than any other single piece of legislation, the G.I. Bill created the basis of today's middle class – well, the white middle class. At the same time, via the Marshall Plan, we re-built war torn nations of millions of non-Americans, including our defeated enemies, some not white.

Almost one million black Americans served honorably in the war, but few saw the benefits of the G.I. Bill, primarily because its programs were administered locally – a key provision put into the law by clever Southern legislators. And private colleges and universities maintained exclusionary admission policies.

The Freedman's Bureau had been designed in 1865 to incorporate four million former slaves into a new, post-war society of 35 million Americans. Likewise, the G.I. Bill was designed in 1944 to re-incorporate 16 million veterans and their families into a new post-war society of 150 million Americans. Just about the same percentages. While the former failed miserably for black Americans, 80 years later, the latter succeeded astoundingly. For white Americans.

As remarkable as was Lincoln's Emancipation Proclamation, it took another 79 years for any President to issue any Executive Order or Proclamation designed to benefit black Americans. In 1942, FDR issued Executive Order 8802 banning racial discrimination by government contractors (all white) who were then awash in billions of government contracts.

The Federal Courts were also of no help to, and too often a hindrance to, black Americans until 1948 when the Supreme Court held in *Shelley v. Kramer* that racial deed restrictions were unconstitutional. Before that, the Court's sad legacy included a series of anti-black American decisions including *Dred Scott v. Sandford* (1857), *U.S. v. Cruikshank* (1876), *Civil Rights Cases* (1883) *Plessy v. Ferguson* (1896) and more. 159 years of Federal judicial protection for white Americans only.

The Civil Rights struggle of the 1960's brought what some call "The Second Reconstruction." While enormous progress was made, and much of it due to affirmative acts of the President, Congress and the Supreme Court, one need only watch or read the news each morning to know that we have much more to do. In 1865, 99.5% of the net worth in the U.S. was owned by white Americans. Today it is 99%.

Democrats Hillary Clinton, Bernie Sanders and Barack Obama all view reparations as politically impractical, polarizing and not a valid policy to pursue. Needless to say, no prominent Republican has spoken in favor.

We have, however, paid "reparations" once – to Japanese Americans interred during WWII. In 1988, the Civil Liberties Act awarded $20,000 to each survivor.

Ironically, the only time the Federal Government ever paid any compensation for slavery was in 1862 when under Lincoln's plan for compensated emancipation in Washington, D.C., approximately $1 million in Federal funds was paid, not to the black slaves themselves, but to the white slave owners for the freedom of 3,185 slaves.

While the wisdom of any form of reparations is best addressed at another time or by others, the most intriguing proposal is that of Harvard Law Professor Charles J. Ogletree, Jr., who thoughtfully proposes a "national program of job training and public works that takes racial justice as its mission but includes the poor of all races." Somehow, such a mandate seems eerily familiar.

As with so many issues, how one stands depends upon where one sits. Perhaps it is time to switch seats.

III. HERITAGE

"THE ARISAKA - FROM TOGO KOGYO TO PHILADELPHIA"[10]

As a young boy growing up in a quiet suburb of New Orleans, I often ventured into a dusty closet in the utility room adjacent to our carport. There, amongst numerous rakes, hoes, brooms, and miscellaneous tools was an out of place item – an implement of war from another time and place. A 7.7 mm, bolt action Japanese Army Type 99 Arisaka rifle.

It is an ominous weapon, yet not the quality of similar U.S. ordinance of its era. In that pre-Sony/Lexus time, "Made in Japan" had a decidedly different meaning than it does today. I often held this rifle for hours on end in my back yard and thought about the men who made it, the man to whom it was issued and who last fired it, and my father, U.S. Marine Corps Corporal Allen Jere Tillery (USMC No. 841175), one of the last men to be at the killing end of it. It inspired me to a life of inquiry about history, war, law, politics and why men act as they do.

Like many Baby Boomers, I often went to bed asking my father, "What did you do in the war, Daddy?" Yes, in the 1950's and even early 1960's "the" War was World War II. Korea was a "police action" and we still had the good sense to have only "advisors" in Vietnam. My father had lots of war stories to tell, as he served in the South Pacific Theatre for 2 ½ years fighting the Japanese Imperial Army at the point.

My brother and I listened wide-eyed to his tales of combat which always ended with him singing a lovely Japanese lullaby as we drifted off. While we dreamed of military adventures, my father prayed that his sons would never have to see what he had at 19 in the stinking jungles and bloody beaches of a half dozen Pacific islands. He always said he fought so we would not have to.

---

[10] The Philadelphia Lawyer, Vol. 77, No. 1, Spring 2014, and reprinted in The Interpreter, Vol. 259, Sept. 1, 2019

This weapon, the Arisaka, which came to inspire me has quite a history. It is named for Colonel Nariakira Arisaka (1852-1915), head of the Japanese commission which directed the development of a new army rifle in the 1890's. It was a considerable advancement over the rifle it replaced, the 8 mm Murata, the first indigenously produced Japanese rifle, in use since 1880. The Empire of Japan, less than 50 years earlier a closed, feudal society, was in the 1890's a rising industrial and military power which would soon, in 1905, shock the world by defeating the once mighty Russian Navy in the Russo-Japanese War. The Land of the Rising Sun had come a long way since 1853 when U.S. Admiral Matthew Perry sailed his "black ships" into Tokyo Bay and compelled that insular nation to open up, or be leveled by cannon fire. It did and Perry's insult was repaid with a vengeance on December 7, 1941.

From 1898 on, Japan produced over 6.4 million of various types of Arisakas before the last few shoddy, "last ditch" versions were cobbled together in July of 1945 from scrap as the Empire collapsed. It was state of the art for a long time, comparable to the British Lee-Enfield, the German Mauser or the American Springfield. It was the primary personal weapon of virtually every Japanese soldier on every God-forsaken island and atoll from Saipan and Tinian to Guam and Iwo Jima. U.S. Marines bearing superior, semi-automatic M-1 Garand rifles or carbines faced off against the Emperor's best bearing Arisakas.

The Arisaka is curious in several respects. Mine bears many scars of battle and has been fired many times, no doubt even killed one or more U.S. troops. The Type 99 includes a flip-down, wire monopod under the barrel to allow the user to steady the weapon to fire in the prone position. Unfortunately, the wire is rather flimsy and provides a wobbly firing platform. Many were removed and discarded as a nuisance in the field. It also has a unique safety, operated by pressing in the large knurled disc at the rear of the bolt and rotating it in a 1/8 clockwise turn. It also includes a rather optimistic, winged, "anti-aircraft" sight which theoretically permits the user to lead a speeding aircraft and shoot it down. Neither Corporal Tillery nor I are aware of any instance of a U.S. aircraft being shot by, much less downed by, an Arisaka. But it could take down a Marine at 400 meters.

The model I have, a Type 99, is so designated by the last two digits of the Japanese year of the reign of the then Emperor, Hirohito. Thus, in Japanese calendar year 2599, or Gregorian calendar year 1939, the Type 99 was first produced.

Though a spoil of war taken from an unwilling donor on the field of battle by a victor, and I having possession, it is, I suppose, technically still the property of the Emperor, now Akihito (son of Hirohito). Each Arisaka was originally stamped on its receiver with the symbol of The Emperor – a 16-petal Chrysanthemum, indicating that it was the property of the Emperor, not the soldier who carried it and not the Imperial Army.

However, only Arisakas, like mine, taken in the field still bear this gentle, but bold symbol. After the war, in one of its final standing orders, the Imperial Army Staff ordered that the Chrysanthemum be ground off all weapons before they were officially surrendered to U.S. forces, as a way of saving face. Short of a personal appeal accompanied by an apology, the Emperor will not be getting my Arisaka back anytime soon.

Mine bears the Chrysanthemum and the Kanji characters Shiki (Type) and Kojuko (99) on the top of the receiver.

九九 式

It also bears a Serial Number with Armory designations:

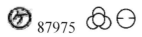

The first small symbol (kana) and number means this rifle was number 87,975 in Series 30, the first series of 100,000

manufactured in 1939, two years before Pearl Harbor and five years before August 15, 1944 when Corporal Tillery acquired it. The second symbol means it was produced at the Togo Kogyo Arsenal. It probably saw lots of action before its bearer met his demise on Tinian in 1944.

This arsenal was operated by a private contractor, Togo Kogyo Co., Ltd., a prominent manufacturer of machine tools and vehicles. It produced 557,000 Type 99 Arisakas between 1939 and 1945. In 1984, the company changed its name to Mazda Motor Corporation, now headquartered in Hiroshima. If I had known the same company that made this rifle also made my 1989 RX-7 sports car, I would have bought a Ford.

It also includes an early model Type 30 Bayonet with a hooked quillion and markings indicating it was manufactured at another arsenal, the Kokura Arsenal in Kokura, Japan.

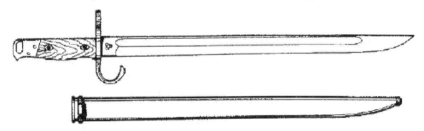

The 16 inch blade includes a "blood gutter." G.I. lore has it that this indentation along the length of the blade allows blood to seep out of a wound preventing a vacuum and permitting the attacker to easily withdraw it from a victim. In reality, it is merely a design feature to enhance strength of the blade. My father says he was taught in boot camp that the quickest way to remove your bayonet from a victim was to pull the trigger. Such was war at the point in 1944.

The ancient Japanese city of Kokura had been the primary target of the second atomic bomb drop ("Fat Man") on August 9, 1945. Major Charles Sweeney turned his B-29, "Bock's Car", towards Nagasaki, his secondary target, when he could not see Kokura, then obscured by clouds and smoke from the recent fire-bombing of nearby Yahata. Kokura had first been spared atomic infamy only three days before when Colonel Paul Tibbitts flying the "Enola Gay" found clear skies above Hiroshima to drop the first atomic bomb ("Little Boy") and needed not visit his secondary target, Kokura. My aunt Xenia Tillery, also a lawyer, tells me her uncle, Sgt. Joseph S. Stiborik was Tibbits' radar operator on that historic mission.

The Enola Gay took off that fateful day, August 6, 1945, at 2:45 AM, from North Field, Tinian Island about a year after the U.S. Marines obliterated a crack Japanese Army defending it. Shortly after the assault troops departed, Corporal Allen J. Tillery, serving as an interpreter with the 8th Marine Regiment Battalion Intelligence Section would encounter the bearer of my Arisaka on the opposite end of the island.

My father had been trained by the Marine Corps to kill Japanese soldiers, but also to speak and read Japanese in order to acquire intelligence from captured troops and often to persuade holdouts in the field to surrender. Today at 86, he still delights in surprising Japanese tourists with his rusty idiom. His vocabulary, however, is decidedly military, so he has to be reminded not to ask waiters at sushi restaurants how many Nambu machine guns are in the kitchen.

Tinian, in The Marianas, an island 12 miles long and 4 miles across was in 1944 defended by 9,000 battle-hardened Japanese Imperial Troops under command of Colonel Kioshi Ogata, a veteran of the Sino-Japanese War. His core 4,000 man 50th Regiment had seen lots of action in Manchuria. Although most perished at hands of U.S. Marine invaders, as many as 800 remained armed and hiding in caves throughout the island, ready to fight to the death for the Emperor. Surrender was disgrace. It was not an option.

It was just such a small group of Japanese soldiers that Corporal Tillery encountered that hot August 1944 day in a cave on the southern end of Tinian Island, in the face of a cliff on the

Karorinasu plateau near Marupo Springs, the scene of fierce fighting not a few weeks before.

Tillery's 15 man patrol had been tasked with killing or capturing the soldiers hiding in the caves who had been firing on truck convoys at the base of the cliffs and whom had recently killed a Navy Sea-Bee driving a truck on the road. Perhaps this was the last kill of my Arisaka. In six months, the patrol would have over 140 encounters with Japanese troops like this first one.

The last shots from my Ariska fired in anger were directed to the point Marine at the head of this patrol on August 15, 1944. Two Japanese soldiers fired, missed and then retreated into the cave.

Corporal Tillery was given the unenviable job of crawling up the cliff to get near the cave to coax its denizens out. In his flawless and distinct Japanese, the Marine Corporal explained that the battle was over, they were surrounded, that if they put down their weapons and exited the cave with hands up, no harm would come to them and that to die now was useless. No sooner had the last foreign word passed the Marine's lips, did the soldiers yell "Banzai!," "Banzai!" and several hand grenades exploded in the cave. One tried to run out with weapon in hand, but was met with a hail of M-1 and Browning Automatic Rifle (BAR) fire.

When the smoke cleared, the distorted bodies of 4 or 5 Japanese soldiers were found near the mouth of the cave. They had committed Seppuku ("stomach-cutting" - the act of the dishonored samurai warrior disemboweling himself with a short sword – a tantō), though with the modern and more effective means of a hand grenade held against the belly.

The cave was filled with supplies, weapons and ammunition. They could have held out and killed more U.S. troops for a long time. In 1965, twenty years after the war ended, two Japanese soldiers wandered out of the jungle on Guam and surrendered to a local policeman.

All of the cave's contents were destroyed except a couple of Arisakas and a Nambu light machine gun which Corporal Tillery took with him. He gave one Arisaka to his tent mate who was an aide to a morale officer, and as such, had connections. The tent mate got a carpenter to build a crate to ship the two souvenirs to his mother in Nashville, Tennessee. She, in turn, shipped the Corporal's Arisaka to his mother (my grandmother) Lake Erie Johnston Tillery, in Shreveport, Louisiana, where the Corporal found it when he returned from war on October 7, 1945, nine years to the day before I was born.

The Corporal or Allen J. as I like to call him, married, moved to suburban New Orleans, and literally hung out his shingle to practice law above a bank on the Mississippi River, near smelly stockyards and an illegal casino. The Arisaka lay in storage, only to be found by my curious little hands at about the age of 10 which began my musings.

Hurricane Betsy hit New Orleans with a vengeance in 1965 and our home was flooded with 6 feet of muck, mire and Gulf water. Like my baseball card collection, my mother's silverware and almost all our household goods, the Arisaka was submerged in this toxic soup for a few days. We survived and rebuilt and I found the Arisaka. It was rusted, inoperable and generally a mess. I was saddened and knew my father would be, too.

I resolved to restore it and present to the Corporal. Though only 11 years old, I was rather handy, a fact which never ceases to amuse my children. I try to explain that facility with mechanical things does not necessarily translate to i-phones and computers.

I worked diligently in secret for several months on my project. When complete, the Arisaka looked almost new, except for the battle scars and was operable. I even bought some ammunition for it, but never did fire it. August 15, 1944, Marupo Springs, Tinian remains the last time and place this killing tool was fired.

When I presented it to the Corporal, I thought I saw a tear in the eye of the old Marine. He proudly kept it visible, near his books, in his library and I often sat holding it there and thinking.

Unbeknownst to me, not a few months before in June 1965, he had completed a manuscript about his war experiences, Well and Smartly Done – A Remembrance of War, 1943-1945. For reasons still unknown to me, he did not show it to me until 20 years later when he inscribed a bound copy, "For Kelly – a codification of all the war stories and sea-tales that you will never have to listen to again." It includes a vivid and detailed description of that fateful day when he acquired the Arisaka.

Fast forward 40 years to late August 2005 – Hurricane Katrina delivers a body blow to the New Orleans area, depositing up to 18 feet of water in my parents' home in Chalmette. Once again, the Arisaka joined their worldly goods under the deluge, this time for weeks.

Allen J. eventually retrieved the Arisaka from its damp and muddy resting place, but reported that it was an ugly, rusty mess. I asked him to ship it to me so I could try to restore it, again, as I had 40 years before. He did and I tried. But it was too far gone. Or at least beyond my humble ability to revive it.

I located a retired Marine, Ronald H. Morgan, near our vacation home in Vermont who restores weapons as a hobby. I brought him the patient and he promised to make it shine. And he did. The Corporal would be pleased.

I shall return to New Orleans soon and present the Arisaka to my father – again. Until then, I still often hold it and think of how grateful I am that some 56 year old Tokyo lawyer, son of a 50th Regiment Japanese soldier, is not sitting in his library holding my father's M-1.

"ON SERVICE"[11]

My son, Alexander, turned 18 in 2012. He is handsome, lean, 6'4", bright and strong. After working out recently on a cruise, a lady with a room near us observed, "He must eat hand grenades for breakfast." Yes, he is an impressive specimen of young manhood. He would make an excellent soldier.

Within 30 days of his 18th birthday, he was required by the 1980 Registration Under Military Selective Service Act to register with the Selective Service System. If he had not registered, he would be denied access to Federal student loans and grants, job training, some government jobs and in some states a driver's license. My daughter, Erin, turned 18 this year. She did not have to register. My other daughter Kate, will turn 18 in two years and, like Erin, will not have to do so, unless the law is changed or found unconstitutional.

The constitutionality of conscription, based on Article I, Section 8, Clause 17 of the Constitution, has been upheld by the Supreme Court in several decisions beginning with Butler v. Perry, 240 U.S. 328 (1916). The Confederacy was the first to pioneer modern conscription on this continent on April 16, 1862, followed shortly thereafter by the Union on August 4, 1862. In 1981, the Court upheld the "female exemption," holding that since the purpose of the law was to prepare for a draft of "combat troops" and since women were excluded from combat, there was a "rational Congressional basis" (an oxymoron?) for the different treatment of women. Rostker v. Goldberg, 435 U.S. 57. The 9th Circuit Court of Appeals is presently considering a new constitutional challenge to this exception in National Coalition For Men v. Selective Service System. Only a few days before that court heard oral argument recently, the Department of Defense announced that after studying the issue for three years, all positions in the U.S. military would be open to women, including combat, no exceptions. The Supreme Court's "rationale" in Rostker thus no longer exists. I fully expect

---

[11] The Philadelphia Lawyer, Vol.78, No. 4, Winter 2015

the 9th Circuit to find the Selective Service "female exception" unconstitutional.

It is my fervent hope that none of my offspring ever have to serve in the military. That is not meant as any negative reflection on the brave men and women who serve or have served in or on our military services themselves, but rather just me being a protective parent. In fact, virtually every male in my family from my Father, Allen J. Tillery, a Marine in WWII, going back to my Great, Great, Great, Great, Great Grandfather, Henry Tillery, in Washington's Continental Army, has served proudly. I am neither proud nor ashamed that I have never served my country, but now regret that I did not. Strange statement from a graduate of Quaker Swarthmore College, a place Nixon derisively called the "Kremlin On The Crum." It is not that I had or have any great desire to shoot or be shot at. And if paying taxes counts as service, I have more than paid my dues. No, I regret two things — missing the discipline and character-building provided only by military service and not having given my time, blood, sweat and tears for a nation that has given me and my family so much.

I actually did serve our Commander in Chief twice, — in 1972, as a Youth Consultant for President Nixon's National Commission on Marijuana and Drug Abuse and in 1978, as a Law Clerk in the U.S. Army Claims Service. Though advising on recreational drug use and evaluating servicemen's claims for damaged household goods hardly count as "service." A friend jokes that I served honorably in The Sexual Revolution, you know, that period between the invention of The Pill (1960) and the appearance of AIDS (1981). But such humor does a disservice to those who served, including many of my forebears.

CONTINENTAL

I have lived in the metropolitan Philadelphia area for over 30 years and am a history buff, but only recently visited George Washington's 1777-78 Headquarters at Valley Forge, where I made a fascinating discovery. I knew that my Great, Great, Great, Great, Great Grandfather, Henry Tillery (c. 1725-1795) and his son, my

Great, Great, Great, Great Grandfather, Joshua Tillery (c. 1745-1820) of Culpepper County, Virginia, both fought the British in The Revolutionary War and were recognized for "Public Service Claims," entitling me and my progeny to Sons of (SAR) or Daughters of The American Revolution (DAR) status.

What I did not know is that another Tillery, their cousin, Lt. John Tillery, of North Carolina, served in Washington's Continental Army and was camped with him that bitter winter, not 25 yards from the great General's Headquarters. The thought that one of my bloodline had been so close to, and no doubt saw and perhaps even met, the Father of Our Country sent shivers down my spine. John Marshall and Alexander Hamilton were there, too. Known in family lore as "Revolutionary John," John Tillery served in the 3rd North Carolina Infantry under Colonel Jethro Sumner, part of McIntosh's Brigade lead by Brigadier-General Lachlan McIntosh, a close confidante of Washington, and part of his 3rd Division under the then 20-year-old Gilbert du Motier, otherwise known as the Marquis de Lafayette. Washington, Lafayette and Tillery. Could not get any better than this for an old history buff!

Drawing upon this association, a century later, my Great Grandfather Tillery had a younger half-brother named Goodwin Lafayette Tillery who served in the Confederate Army, Alabama 23rd Infantry, Co. I. Uncle Goodwin, as my Father knew him, reportedly carried cannonballs to Rebel batteries up Lookout Mountain at the battle of the same name (Nov. 24, 1863). Later known affectionately as "Old Coot," Uncle Goodwin attended one of the last great gatherings of Confederate Civil War veterans in Shreveport, La. in 1936. My Father, who would go to war himself only seven years later, rode in a parade with the old, bearded vet as other old men who had once been slaves looked on silently from the roadside.

DEUTSCHLAND UBER ALLES

Although I know little of the military exploits, if any, of my maternal ancestors, I do know that my Mother's father, my Grandfather, Irvin Joseph George Janssen, of pure Teutonic heritage, fought against his own people, Le Boche, in France as part of the U.S. Army Air Corps in WWI. While in later years he claimed to have engaged Baron von Richtofen, The Red Baron, in dog fights, official records reflect that he only repaired and maintained the flying machines of some who may have.

The only other maternal forbear of which I know, also a Hun, had quite a different 'military' experience. Family lore has it that Frederick David Decker (1849-1905), my Great Grandfather emigrated to New Orleans in the late 1860's to avoid the draft of The Iron Chancellor, Otto von Bismarck, who was then consolidating modern Germany and crushing the French at Sedan in the brief, and ill-conceived (at least for the French), Franco – Prussian War. (1870-71)

Curiously, one of the few items Frederick David brought with him on his long journey to the Crescent City, besides his cigar-making tools, was a small bust of Bismarck. It sat on my Grandmother's and later my Mother's mantle for years and I always admired it and appreciated its irony. It inspired my first college history paper, "Otto Von Bismarck and the Constitution of the North German Confederation" (1972), and my Mother gave it to me as a law school graduation gift in 1979. It has a prominent place in my home today – a symbol of one man's determination to avoid the idiocy of war.

"WINNING" THE LOTTERY

It also reminds me of my own brush with the possibility of involuntary induction. In 1972, as I turned 18, there was still a real draft, we still had 24,000 troops in Vietnam, and I was issued a draft lottery number. My older brother had already had one for two years. Fortunately, we both had high numbers, and Henry Kissinger, pre-election, had announced, "Peace is at hand," however disingenuously. As it turned out, I was in jeopardy for only a few months, as on January 27, 1973, Secretary of Defense Melvin R. Laird announced the end of the draft and the creation of all-volunteer armed services.

"O CANADA!"

Although none in our household supported this war, my Father, who had served bravely in the U.S. Marine Corps for 2½ years in the South Pacific in WWII, was adamant that if our country called, it was our duty to serve, even if it meant going to Vietnam. My Mother, on the other hand, was equally adamant that if we were called, she was going to follow her Grandfather Frederick David's tradition of resisting tyrants and take us to Canada. If I had been forced to emigrate to The Great White North, I am certain I would not have taken a bust of Tricky Dick. Perhaps a bobble head.

Fortunately, even though "peace" was still three long and painful years away, we were de-escalating and the clash of parental philosophies never had to be resolved. I was particularly pleased since both parents, to this day, say it is the one issue that could have broken their marriage. And I really do not understand ice hockey. In New Orleans we put ice in our Mint Juleps; we did not skate on it.

My Father's older brother, James Henry Tillery, Jr. (1920-1991), also a Marine, served with President Roosevelt's son, James, in Carlson's Raiders, the famous "Gung Ho" unit which made the first U.S. land attack on Japanese forces at Makin Atoll in August 1942. Although their father, James H. Tillery, Sr., (1888-1952) never served in the military, he provided valuable public service as "Captain Jim," a fire captain in Shreveport, LA for many years.

"CONFEDERATES IN MY ATTIC"

His father, however, Milton Jared Tillery (1834-1909) served 1491 days in the Confederate Army in a storied Texas cavalry unit, known as The W.P. Lane Rangers. The exploits of his unit are painstakingly recorded in an oft-cited work of one of his comrades, William Williston Heartsill in <u>Fourteen Hundred And Ninety One Days In The Confederate Army</u>. (1867-Original Handpress; 1954, McCowat-Mercer Press; 1992, Broadfoot Publishing).

Private Tillery and his unit were captured by the forces of General John A. McClernand, part of General William Tecumseh Sherman's army, on January 12, 1863 at the Battle of Arkansas Post. He and 4,000 Confederates repulsed 60,000 Yankees on six frontal assaults succumbing to their overwhelming numbers only on the seventh.

The Rangers were taken prisoner and shipped north to Camp Butler, Illinois for internment. But on April 7, 1863, they were transported to City Point, Virginia for a prisoner exchange. On April 14, 1863, Milton Jared was exchanged for a Federal prisoner and was once again a free man. After a short stint at Chancellorsville, one in General Braxton Bragg's Army and medical leave in Atlanta, Private Tillery, Private James W. Young and Sgt. James M. Vaughn decide to take "French leave" and return to their old unit.

On their trek home, on May 6, 1863, Milton Jared and his confreres slept in the hallways of the Virginia State Capitol in Richmond designed by Thomas Jefferson, just as Lincoln, only 106 miles away in the War Department Telegraph Office received the news that Lee had decisively defeated Hooker at Chancellorsville and cried, "My God! My God! What will the country say?! What will the country say?!" Less than two years later on April 4, 1865 Lincoln would enter the Confederate Capital triumphantly and sit at Jefferson Davis's desk.

Milton Jared and the Arkansas Post Boys hurried to the outskirts of Richmond to stop Stoneman's raid and to hold off any of Hooker's troops if they got past Lee. Robert E. made sure they did not, but sadly lost his right arm, Stonewall Jackson in the fight.

After walking 736 miles (a particular indignity for a cavalry soldier), they reported back to the W.P. Lane Rangers, then, ironically, guarding Federal prisoners at Camp Ford, Tyler, Texas.

General U.S. Grant disfavored prisoner exchanges for just this reason — the Confederacy had fewer military age men and to return them to fight again seemed absurd. Milton Jared was one of the last Confederates exchanged. Just six weeks later, on May 25, 1863, Lincoln stopped such exchanges because the Confederacy refused to exchange black Federal soldiers. Milton Jared got out in the nick of time.

Although The Rangers saw a little more action, they were disbanded on May 20, 1865 at Sterling, Texas after hearing that Confederate forces under General Joe Johnston had surrendered. Actually, the last intact Confederate army, the 43,000-man force of General Edmund Kirby Smith, surrendered six days later on May 26, 1865, 188 miles away in Shreveport, Louisiana, where my Father would be born 60 years later. I was amused in 1970 when my brother, a new freshman at LSU, moved into a dormitory named for this Rebel General — Kirby Smith Hall.

Milton Jared returned to Panola County, Texas, homesteaded 625 acres and never spoke of his Civil War experiences. His personal copy of Heartsill's book was found among his effects upon his death in 1909.

Six of his eight brothers fought for the same cause, as did almost 100 other Tillery relatives. Their grandfather, William Henry Tillery (1773-1813) of Putnam County, GA was a veteran of the Northwest Indian War (1785-1795), a war brought to an end by local Pennsylvania hero, General "Mad" Anthony Wayne's decisive victory at The Battle of Fallen Timbers.

MORE THAN ONE WAY TO SERVE

Am beginning to feel like Lieutenant Dan in "Forrest Gump", albeit with forebears who fought, but survived their service. With my heritage one might expect more desire to serve and to require others to do so. While that ship has sailed for me, I do favor a national, without exception (other than real physical/mental disability), two year public service requirement in either the military or other public service such as Americorps. Requiring such service anytime between 18 and 25 would provide jobs, man power, pride, discipline, honor and an investment. It also just might make us think more carefully, or at least differently, about putting the "boots" of our sons and daughters "on the ground" in foreign lands. William James first proposed a program of compulsory national service in his 1916 essay, "The Moral Equivalent of War." Time Magazine proposed such a national service system in 2008, and New York Times columnist David Brooks only recently proposed one.

Korean War veteran Congressman Charles Rangel (D-NY) has introduced a Universal National Service Act several times, most recently in 2010. It was voted on only once and defeated in the House – 400 to 2.

In 21 years AmeriCorps, the nation's main public service program has given almost one million young people the opportunity to serve without joining the military, though its funding has repeatedly been cut in recent years.

In the political thriller film, "The Ides of March," Ryan Gosling advises candidate George Clooney to push a mandatory youth national service program, arguing that those who would serve cannot yet vote and that those who would benefit would be too old to qualify — a perfect political program!

I would have my son and daughters sign up with honor, to such a program. After all, they would not be able to vote until the day they would be required to serve.

And they say you cannot control your teenagers.

"NINE IN TIME"

In every American military conflict, siblings and cousins have served together in the same branches, sometimes in the same unit, and sometimes in the same battles. The Battle of Gettysburg and The Civil War were no different. Well, perhaps so in one way. It may be the only American war in which close relatives, even brothers, actually fought on opposite sides.

Taking sibling rivalry to a new level, Private John Wesley Culp (2d Virginia, Co. B) of Gettysburg faced off against his brother William (87th Pennsylvania, Co. E) twice - at the Battle of Falling Waters (July 1, 1861) and again at the Second Battle of Winchester (June 13-15, 1863). Perhaps, thankfully, William was not at Gettysburg only a few weeks later on Day Three, when Wesley was mortally wounded by Union fire not far from where both boys grew up and the famous hill named for their Uncle Henry. Some call it The Brothers War.

Three brothers, also originally from Gettysburg, Robert Newton, Francis Williams "Frank" and Wesley Atwood Hoffman, moved to Virginia in 1856, but returned that steamy July, 1863 in Confederate uniforms. Wes Culp had been an apprentice in their father's Gettysburg carriage shop.

Two other brothers opposed each other at Gettysburg. Union Corporal Rudolph Schwartz (45th New York, 5th German Rifles) from New York City fought on Day One, only to find his brother amongst Confederates captured at the McLean Barn. As his brother was taken behind the lines, Rudolph was killed by a Rebel Minié ball. Though brief, it was their first reunion since leaving Germany. And their last.

While the Culp Brothers' internecine conflict has some degree of notoriety, several sets of brothers fought at Gettysburg on the same side. The most famous, due in large part to the post-war, relentless self-promotion of one, were the Chamberlain Brothers of the 20th Maine, Joshua Lawrence, John and Thomas, who tenaciously held Little Round Top on Day Two.

Nearby, Confederate Colonel William Calvin Oates, commanded the 15th Alabama Infantry as it surged up Little Round Top challenging the Chamberlains where his brother John was mortally wounded. In the early 1900's William tried to have a memorial to his sibling and his unit erected there, but was not allowed to do so.

Confederate Major John Marion Bradley and brother Second Lieutenant George W. Bradley, of the 13th Mississippi, fought valiantly under Brigadier General William Barksdale in and around the Peach Orchard on Day Two, but both met their maker on that bloody Pennsylvania field. Their only other and younger brother Joseph L. Bradley had perished at the Battle of Malvern Hill the year before. There is no record that Mrs. Bradley received condolences from C.S.A. President Jefferson Davis.

Of the 4,000 sons of Michigan at Gettysburg, John Ryder (24th Michigan) and his older brother Alfred (1st Michigan Cavalry) were two fatalities out of the 1,100 Wolverine State casualties.

Minnesota brothers Patrick Henry and Isaac (Ike) Taylor (1st Minnesota, Co. E.), teachers in civilian life, defended the center of the Union Line on Cemetery Ridge on Day Two against Wright's Brigade's famous assault. Only Patrick Henry survived.

In that same confrontation, Colonel George H. Ward led the 15th Massachusetts Infantry, including his brother Lt. Henry C. Ward facing off against the 3rd Georgia at the Emmittsburg Road. George had lost his left leg below the knee at the Battle of Ball's Bluff (October 21, 1861), but late on Day Two, a Confederate ball shattered his right leg. Brother Henry got him to a surgeon, but too late.

Before Lincoln's famous letter of condolence to Mrs. Lydia Bixby about the sacrifice of her five sons (11-21-1864); before the five Sullivan brothers perished together when the USS Juneau was torpedoed (11-15-1942); before nineteen Boys of Bedford,

Virginia died on Omaha Beach (6-6-1944); before Private First Class James Francis Ryan (Matt Damon) lost three brothers in "Saving Private Ryan" (1998); and long before the U.S. Government's "Sole Survivor" deployment policy (1948) designed to prevent such multiple family tragedies...

Nine of my Tillery forebears fought at Gettysburg. As traitors. In Robert E. Lee's vaunted Army of Northern Virginia.

At Oak Ridge, Culp's Hill, McPherson's Ridge, Devil's Den, the Wheatfield, the Slaughter Pen, Rose's Woods, the Peach Orchard, Houck's Ridge, South Cavalry Field, Cemetery Hill and Cemetery Ridge, a Tillery was there. At least one. Sometimes seven or eight.

In 1972, a seventeen year old Louisiana born and bred civilian boy, I crossed the Pennsylvania state line by Chevy via I-95 near Chester at the invitation of the Admissions Committee of Swarthmore College. At the time and until only recently, I thought myself the first Tillery to visit the Keystone State or even to have the courage to venture above the Mason-Dixon Line.

Little did I know, ninety-one years earlier, nine of my relatives, including three Great Grand Uncles marched into Pennsylvania from Virginia through Maryland, uninvited, armed and part of what Gettysburg College Professor Allen C. Guelzo calls "The Last Invasion."

All nine fought and lost, but survived to fight again. And again. And sometimes, again. Two eventually surrendered to General Ulysses S. Grant at Appomattox Court House on April 9, 1865 - Sgt. Lindsay Marion Tillery (3rd Alabama, Co. L.) and Regimental Musician William Henry Tillery (3rd Georgia, Co. F.)

Twenty year old cousin Private Hugh Taylor Tillery (3rd Arkansas, Co. F.) would have been there with his regiment to do so, as well, but he bought the farm at the Battle of Chickamauga only ten weeks after Gettysburg on September 20, 1863. His 3rd Arkansas fought in over thirty engagements from the Battle of Cheat

Mountain (September 12-15, 1861) to Appomattox (April 9, 1865). His regiment lost 282 of 479 men in the fight for Devil's Den on Day Two. Of 119 men of Hugh Taylor's Company F, only ten remained to be paroled by General Grant at war's end.

Great Grand Uncle John Bunyan Tillery escaped back to Virginia via Maryland with the rest of Lee's Army, but expired the next year at only twenty-two in an Atlanta hospital due to a leg wound requiring amputation. His older brother, my Great Grandfather, Milton Jared Tillery, on his 1,077 mile walk from one of the last prisoner exchanges at City Point, Virginia (April 15, 1863) back to rejoin his unit in Tyler, Texas, visited with John Bunyan in that hospital in August 1863. Milton Jared, a cavalry soldier in the "W.P. Lane Rangers" (2nd Regiment, Texas Mounted Rifles, Co. F) had been captured on January 12, 1863 by overwhelming Union forces under Lincoln friend, lawyer and political General John McClernand, at the Battle of Arkansas Post. Unsurprisingly, violating the terms of his parol/exchange, Milton Jared re-joined his unit in December 1863 and fought on until finally surrendering on May 20, 1865 at Sterling, Texas.

Two other of their brothers fought for The Lost Cause – Jonathan Henry Tillery and Goodwin Lafayette Tillery, both of the 23rd Alabama, Co. B. In 1936, my then eleven year old Father, Allen Jere Tillery, rode with his Great Uncle Goodwin Lafayette (a/k/a "Old Coot") in a parade at the 46th National United Confederate Veterans Reunion in Shreveport, Louisiana, past several old black men who had been slaves. The war was not so long ago.

Brother James Burrell Tillery, served in another Alabama Infantry, but was "lost" a common Civil War plight, at Owensburg, Kentucky in 1864 at age of 28.

All nine Tillery Gettysburg combatants descended from Job Tillery (b. <1692, Richmond (Old Rappahannock County), VA), of pure Scottish heritage. Job's progeny, like most of the fiercely independent Scottish frontiersmen of the day, picked up and moved on when settlements grew, south and west to North Carolina (including Tillery, North Carolina), then Georgia, then Alabama, then Arkansas, to Texas, spreading Tillery DNA throughout the Deep South. Although several Tillerys, including my GGGG Grandfather Henry Tillery and his son, my GGG Grandfather Joshua Tillery, Sr., fought in the Revolutionary War to create the Union, over 90 Tillerys, including These Gettysburg Nine, fought to destroy it.

WRIGHT'S BRIGADE – THE "ORIGINAL" HIGH WATERMARK OF THE CONFEDERACY

Wright's Brigade, led by Brigadier General Ambrose Ransom Wright, was part of Major General Richard Heron Anderson's Division of Lt. General A.P. Hill's Third Army Corps. It consisted of several regiments, including the 3rd Georgia Infantry under Colonel Edward J. Walker. Company F, known as "Wilkinson's Rifles," from Wilkinson County, Georgia, including Regimental Musician William Henry Tillery who had just turned 52, only three years younger than General Lee.

The 3rd Georgia Infantry fought in over fifty engagements, from South Mills (April 19, 1862) to Appomattox (April 9, 1865). While the oldest Tillery at Gettysburg, William Henry, as part of Wright's Brigade, advanced about 600 yards from the Confederate lines on Seminary Ridge to help cover the retreat of the remnants of Pickett's Division on July 3, 1863, no Tillery was actually part of "Pickett's Charge" that day. As Regimental Musician, William Henry Tillery was amongst those who astoundingly, 49 years before the sinking of the Titanic, played "Nearer My God To Thee" as the few of Pickett's men left sadly stumbled back to the safety of Seminary Ridge. Perhaps General Robert E. Lee was right when he said, "I don't think we could have had an army without music."

But the day before Pickett's unforgettable charge, Wright's Brigade (sans Wright himself) and William Henry Tillery actually made a successful charge to the low stone wall south of The Angle and almost to the crest of Cemetery Ridge – The "Original" High Water Mark of the Confederacy! Late afternoon, Day Two, saw William Henry's Co. F advance over that same mile of open ground from Seminary Ridge, to the Codori Farm, across the Emmitsburg Road, to the stone wall of Cemetery Ridge and, some say, beyond. The 3rd Georgia Battle Flag was planted near the ridge and several pieces of Union artillery were captured. Not far away, Union Commander General George Gordon Meade himself watched the action sitting astride "Old Baldy" and enjoying a snort of whiskey from the flask of his friend, John Newton, on the low crest of the ridge, behind four belching Union Parrot Rifles. Unfortunately, Wright's men were both ahead of their time and their support troops, left and right. Isolated, in an advanced position, with no flanking support, they were forced to withdraw and abandon their prizes and the high ground. 219 of the 3rd Georgia's 441 fell that day. A lost opportunity soon to be attempted again in less than eighteen hours, but by Pickett, Pettigrew and Trimble. And even less successfully!

General Wright's Brigade, and at least one Tillery, had reached further into Yankee lines and territory than any other – not far from General Meade's Headquarters in the widow Leister's House. One can only imagine what they would have thought if they had realized they were fighting on land owned by a free black man, Abraham Brien.

When asked what chance Pickett had to take Cemetery Ridge on Day Three, Wright told Lt. Colonel Porter Alexander, "Well … it is mostly a question of supports. It is not as hard to get there as it looks. I was there yesterday with my brigade. The real difficulty is to stay there after you get there – for the whole infernal Yankee army is up there in a bunch."

Forgetting his annihilation of Ambrose Burnside's forces trying a similar move at Fredericksburg not seven months before, General Lee was inspired by Wright's near victory to order the fateful attack at the same point the next day with about 15,000 men under Generals Pickett, Pettigrew and Trimble.

Colonel Claiborne Snead of the 3rd Georgia, speaking at a Reunion of the 3rd Georgia in Union Point, GA eleven years later said that he met General Lee after the war in Augusta, Georgia on

March 30, 1870, and when he mentioned the 3rd Georgia, tears gathered in Lee's eyes as he said, "Ah, I remember them well, they were part of Wright's Brigade. Say to them that I shall never cease to love them."

So, it would not be unfair to say that William Henry Tillery was there, at the original "High Water Mark" of the Confederacy and that his unit's near success on Day Two inspired Lee's fateful decision the next day that doomed the Army of Northern Virginia and, indeed, the Confederacy. Guess this Regimental Musician wasn't just whistling "Dixie."

Yet another cousin, Private Hugh Taylor Tillery of the "Hot Spring Hornets" – Co. F, 3rd Arkansas Infantry under Colonel Vannoy Hartog Manning, as part of General John Bell Hood's Texas Brigade, was engaged in intense fighting in Rose's Woods, near Devil's Den on Day Two, one of the first units engaged on Day Two and late the next day at South Cavalry Field repulsing Farnsworth's Charge in one of the last engagements of the battle.

O'NEAL'S BRIGADE

On Day One, at Oak Hill, seven Tillery's fought in three different infantry regiments in Major General Robert Emmett Rode's Division – five in the "Dixie Eagles," Co. L. of the 3rd Alabama Infantry in O'Neal's Brigade – Private John Bunyan Tillery, Sgt. Lindsey Marion Tillery, 2d Corporal Virgil Harrison Tillery, Private Luisey M. Tillery and Private Jonathan P. Tillery. Virgil must have been the regimental mascot as he was only fifteen and his nickname was "Pet." Unfortunately, Colonel Edward Ashbury O'Neil was a better politician than military leader. He misdirected his troops into a powerful Yankee line under General Henry Baxter which drove them into retreat. In less than thirty minutes of 350 men in the 3rd Alabama, 91 were lost on the McClean farm.

Poor leadership likewise befell the other two Tillerys on the field that day. Also there in Rode's Division, in a brigade under Brigadier General Alfred Iverson, Jr., were cousins Corporal

Henry Lee Tillery. (12th North Carolina, Co. G.) and Epaphroditus "Eppy" P. Tillery (5th North Carolina, Co. I.). Iverson directed his troops across Forney's Field into the Yankee line without advance reconnaissance and skirmishers. Within just a few minutes, two-thirds of Iverson's Brigade were casualties.

"Eppy" Tillery of the "Gates County Minutemen" – Co. I, 5th North Carolina Infantry, under Captain Speight Brock West also fought alongside his five cousins of the 3rd Alabama in Rode's Assault on Oak Ridge, including when they cleared Oak and McPherson's Ridges of Yankees. He again joined them the next day in Rode's assault on East Cemetery Hill. And, finally, under new and improved leadership of General Iverson, he helped turn the tide against the Yankees on July 6, 1863 in unusual urban warfare at the First Battle of Hagerstown. His 5th North Carolina fought in over thirty engagements, from First Manasass (July 21, 1861) to Appomattox, surrendering to General Grant at Appomattox Court House on April 9, 1865.

Corporal Henry Lee Tillery of Co. G, 12th North Carolina Infantry under Lt. Colonel William S. Davis also fought alongside his cousins of the 3rd Alabama and the 5th North Carolina, at Oak Ridge. On July 1, Colonel Davis' bold decision to lead a charge of the 12th North Carolina collapsed Union General Baxter's lines and earned high praise from his Division Commander, Major General Robert Emmett Rodes.

Thus, it appears that a Tillery may have been one of the youngest (Virgil Harrison -15) and one of the oldest (William Henry - 52) soldiers in the battle. Although some were as young as 12 and some, reportedly as old as 80, the average age of the combatants was 25.

So, we may conclude that eight of the nine Tillerys at Gettysburg were successful on Day One of the battle. They survived and drove the enemy from their positions. Unfortunately, for them, it would be a three day battle and superior position, resources and, arguably, leadership, would trump their passion and drive them and their revered General Lee from the field and Pennsylvania and the North forever.

Not without some irony, a Tillery returned to Gettysburg 150 years later. My son, Alexander Benjamin Tillery, like his father, born in New Orleans, matriculated at Gettysburg College in 2013.

IV. THE PRACTICE

"BACKSTAGE WITH ROCK N. ROLL, ESQ."[12]

Last week, in my dentist's office, amongst old *People* magazines, I ran across the November 2009 *Rolling Stone* (#1092), celebrating the 25th Anniversary of the Rock and Roll Hall of Fame, featuring a superb cover photograph of rock legends Mick Jagger, Bruce Springsteen and Bono. Although I was the drummer for a short-lived garage band, "The Coldwater Conspiracy," I never made "the cover of Rolling Stone," (Dr. Hook and the Medicine Show), though I did once get a Letter To the Editor printed (RS 9/8/88); however, I have represented over 50 artists who have, including those three – Michael Phillip Jagger ("Mick"), Bruce Frederick Joseph Springsteen ("The Boss") and Paul David Hewson ("Bono Vox").

In 32 years of my Philadelphia-based, intellectual property practice I have represented almost every top musical artist one can imagine, from Meatloaf to Madonna, Michael Jackson to Milli Vanilli, The Who to U2 and scores of others. As a frequent client, The Grateful Dead, would say, "Oh, what a long, strange trip it has been."

I am often asked, especially by law students and young lawyers, "How did you get such an interesting practice?" "And how can I get in on it?" Well, first, it was not a result of my drumming skills. I am no Keith Moon or Stewart Copeland. Though I did see Keith play (and destroy) his drums in 1968 and later represented The Who and The Police.

No, my career move into the strange world of rock'n'roll law came, as such things often do, entirely fortuitously. I was a young associate in a storied Philadelphia law firm handling a wide variety of litigation matters. Sure, I had studied copyright law at Penn and still liked to play my drums, but I did not have any

---

[12] The Philadelphia Lawyer, Vol. 75, No. 1, Spring 2012 and reprinted on Domaintimes.Info

interest in or opportunity to use these experiences in the legal arena and never expected to do so.

Opportunity knocked one day. A partner came into my office and said, "Hey, I heard you are a bright guy and a drummer. Can you handle a trademark case for Black Sabbath?" Imagine my surprise and delight. "Of course," I said. So he dumped a file on my desk and left.

I knew nothing of trademark law. But, a fast learner, I knew an opportunity when I saw one. Black Sabbath had only recently fired Ozzy Osborne due to his substance abuse problems. Curiously, I would later represent Ozzy after he made a comeback courtesy of his new manager, and later, wife, Sharon.

This was 1980, the beginning of the rock merchandising revolution. Although Elvis and The Beatles had exploited their names and likenesses, the explosion of rock merchandising, particularly t-shirts, did not occur until the late 1970's, coincidentally, just as I began my legal career.

As luck would have it, the originator and leader of this nascent and booming industry, Winterland Productions, of San Francisco, was represented by Michael L. Krassner, Esq., an old friend of the partner who had brought me the Black Sabbath file. The incredible and rapid success of the business inevitably attracted imitators, those who sought "to reap where they had not sown," – known in the industry, euphemistically, as "bootleggers." At virtually every concert around the country, young men carrying bags or bundles of counterfeit t-shirts bearing the names and trademarks of the artist(s) then playing in the nearby venue would roam the parking lots selling their fake wares to eager, bargain-hunting concert-goers. Such faux items were less expensive and of lesser quality than the authentic wares sold only inside the venue. The bootleggers did not pay license fees, taxes, vendor fees or, for that matter, legal fees. Each illegal sale made outside meant one less sale of the legitimate goods inside, thus depriving the concessionaire, the merchandising company, and the artist(s) of substantial revenue.

Since it was not unusual for bands to make on tour as much, and sometimes more, in merchandising revenue as in ticket revenue, something had to be done. In early 1979, Krassner initiated a legal strategy to enforce the rights of Winterland's artist clients seeking and securing injunctions with orders of seizure to prevent the sale of counterfeit merchandise.

While most know that Philadelphia has a special place in the pantheon of rock music – American Bandstand, The Philadelphia Sound, Live Aid, etc., few know that it has also been the hotbed of music merchandise counterfeiting. Perhaps it is because of its central east coast location and/or its plethora of enterprising and less than savory characters.

I passed the bar in October 1979 and in 1980, secured my first such Order to protect Black Sabbath. Originally, we had to secure individual orders in every city where a band played. However, we soon developed two innovative injunctions that were less costly and more efficient. We secured many Facility/Venue Permanent Injunctions and Seizure Orders in the name of the venue concessionaire. Such an Order could be used to protect the sales of merchandise of any performer(s) appearing in the venue. And we created the Permanent Tour Injunction and Seizure Order to protect an artist on an entire tour. Both worked well and soon became industry standards.

Based on repeated successes, I became National Litigation Counsel for Winterland. This required me to travel around the country with scores of artists on tour seeking court orders in over 35 states. While my experiences hardly rival those of Pamela Des Barres (I'm With the Band), or Cameron Crowe (Almost Famous), I had some interesting adventures "on the road."

Although I was to represent The Grateful Dead many times over the years, the first time produced the most interesting encounter. In 1980 Jimmy Carter was seeking reelection and The Dead were playing several dates at The Spectrum. Carter was soon to visit Philadelphia and several of his clean cut, young advance men were in town staying near The Dead at the Warwick Hotel. The

Dead invited them backstage and to the after-party. Late that night, after securing all the confiscated counterfeit Dead paraphernalia, I joined The Dead, the Carter men and other associated hangers on and groupies at the party.

As the only attendee in a suit, I stood out as much as the Georgia boys. While chatting with them about the campaign, I noticed some activity on a nearby coffee table that was not entirely legal, and it was not trademark counterfeiting. As a good Democrat, I quietly suggested that it might not be a good idea for them to remain. They downed their beers (<u>not</u> "Billy Beer", as I recall), thanked me and took off, avoiding a potential scandal. Just the year before, a Special Counsel had been appointed to investigate whether Carter Chief of Staff, Hamilton Jordan, had sniffed cocaine at Studio 54.

It was not all sex, drugs and rock'n'roll, however. There was tragedy, too. I represented Bruce Springsteen many times and was backstage at The Spectrum on December 8, 1980, the night John Lennon was killed. Bruce was on stage and about to come off when we heard the sad news. Jon Landau, Bruce's manager, insisted that no one say a word to Bruce or the band since they had to play two encores. So the backstage entourage had to watch Bruce and the band come off their concert high with smiles, and high fives and down Gatorade while a couple of dozen people stood around somberly, some trying to hold back tears. Twice. After the second encore, Landau pulled Bruce aside, put his arm around his shoulder and walked him down a hallway. As they receded into the bowels of The Spectrum, we watched Bruce slump when told. The next night, Bruce dedicated his show to Lennon saying, "Without him, we would not be here."

I had been a lawyer less than a year and I was representing "the future of rock'n'roll" on "the night the music died."

There was tragedy on yet another night. I was representing Bob Dylan and The Grateful Dead at a huge J.F.K. Stadium show in 1987. Unbeknownst to all, this was to be the last event held in this legendary Philadelphia venue. Even though another client, The Rolling Stones, were to play there soon thereafter, the crumbling condition of the stadium prompted then-Mayor Wilson Goode to close the facility permanently.

But that was not the tragedy, at least not the human one. The man who "discovered" Dylan (and many others), John H. Hammond, of Columbia Records, died that day, July 10, 1987. As I sat backstage with my security team cooling off, everyone, even the crew, was crushed up against the stage as The Dead were finishing up their last of one of their legendary, never-ending encores. We were virtually alone as a trailer door opened behind us and a man stumbled out and almost fell on my security man, startling him to the point that he reacted with raised, clenched fist. I quickly restrained him as I recognized it was Dylan himself. As a roadie whisked Dylan off, I realized that he was no doubt distraught at the loss of his mentor. I am glad I did not have to explain how my famous client had come to get a bloody nose courtesy of my security.

With J.F.K. Stadium condemned, The Rolling Stones had to quickly, and at considerable expense, reconfigure their stage for Veterans Stadium. As with all tours, the band had insurance with a "no play" clause to protect from the expense of such unexpected occurrences. Lloyds of London refused to honor the claim and I was engaged by The Stones to sue. The matter was ultimately resolved amicably, prior to Mick having to be deposed. But I did get a kick out of having the phone number of his home on the island of Mustique.

Yes, there were lots of groupies, too. I will always remember the one who ran naked backstage insisting she had to see Jerry Garcia. When someone asked me what to do, I gave him counterfeit t-shirt, told him to put it on her and escort her out. I don't know if she ever found Jerry.

And there, of course, were drugs. I remember fighting to avoid a contact high from vast clouds of smoke backstage at a Lynyrd Skynyrd concert in Saratoga Springs, N.Y. Roadies were amused when I told them I had once worked for President

Nixon's National Commission on Marijuana and Drug Abuse. As a Youth Consultant, <u>not</u> a "tester."

And there was lots of incredible rock'n'roll. I saw hundreds of incredible performances, usually from only a few feet away. And once I even got to sit in on the drums with the instrument techies from Oasis. Heady stuff.

Lawyers representing famous people, have the added perk of frequent and widespread publicity. As my country-lawyer father always says, "For a lawyer, any publicity is good publicity, as long as they spell your name right and the word 'indicted' is not in the same sentence." From <u>The Legal Intelligencer</u> to <u>The National Law Journal</u>, from local network TV affiliates to live with Bob Schieffer at Live Aid on the CBS Morning News, I received a lot of press. One reporter gave me the moniker "Mr. Search and Seizure."

Finally, I played a small part in the "Cherry Garcia" story. When Ben & Jerry first came out with this flavor without securing Jerry Garcia's approval, I brought it to the attention of Krassner who notified Harold Kant, The Dead's personal counsel. Kant secured a licensing deal which is, I understand, still a large source of revenue for the Garcia Estate. "Cherry Garcia" has long been and remains the number one selling Ben and Jerry's flavor.

I spent a large part of my first 20 years of my law practice servicing this industry. But like most things, it changed, much of the work became commoditized, and I moved on to protecting intellectual property rights of clients in a myriad of other, mostly more high tech industries. But I will always think fondly of my time in the world of rock'n'roll.

"EVERYONE IS ENTITLED TO INTELLECTUAL PROPERTY PROTECTION"[13]

When I was a young associate with a large Philadelphia law firm in 1980, I got my first secretary. It was the luxury era of IBM Selectric typewriters in which each lawyer, including associates, had his/her own secretary. Before I met her, the office manager alerted me that she looked just like Sophia Loren. And she did. Turns out that she was also an outstanding secretary and eventually, a good friend. But she had a past which she sheepishly disclosed to me one day almost out of the blue. She had worked for years for a then elderly, prominent Philadelphia lawyer who I had encountered on occasion. She was his typist for his secret "hobby" writing steamy, pornographic novels and stories. She was amused by my then wild and carefree yuppie bachelor life in Center City, but her past explained why she blushed at nothing I told her.

I was bemused but thought no more of this curious experience of my new assistant until a few years later by which time I had started my own firm with two partners and my secretary. I got a call from a gentleman who said he was an advisor to many businesses. When I asked what kind, he simply said, "adult." My secretary laughed when told and said her experience might be very helpful to these new clients.

So in my first foray into the world of "adult" businesses, I was asked to represent the "Adult Entertainment Coalition", a group of Pennsylvania businesses who sought to challenge a new law which restricted the manner in which adult films could be shown. The coalition's advisor had come to me as a result of seeing press reports about some of my victories in intellectual property cases on behalf of famous musical artists. I guess he thought if I could protect the intellectual property of Madonna, I could do the same for Marilyn Chambers. Well, I did once represent Barenaked Ladies.

---

[13] The Philadelphia Lawyer, Vol. 78, No. 2, Summer 2015

Anyway, I was somewhat leery and knew my more conservative partners would be concerned, so I asked for a huge retainer. To my surprise and delight, a check appeared the next morning. Although I tried mightily to craft a viable theory under Federal Copyright Law to undermine this Puritanical Pennsylvania law, it was simply not possible. Cognizant of the admonition of J. Paul Getty to his lawyers, "Don't tell me I can't do what I want to do. Tell me how I can do what I want to do," I hesitated to tell my new clients that I could not accomplish what they wanted me to. Businessmen so often see lawyers as impediments, naysayers. But, as we sometimes must, I said no. So I sent the Coalition my opinion letter and a firm check for more than half of the retainer which I had not had to use.

My new clients were stunned. Not that a lawyer had told them they could not do what they wanted to do (and without a "how to" either), but that a lawyer would return any part of a retainer, much less more than half.

This led to a plethora of more clients and matters in almost every aspect of the "adult industry." Only recently, that same advisor observed, in connection with a new case, "Win, lose or draw; you are still the best. I am certain of this. The first time I met you, you didn't tell me what I wanted to hear but I knew what you told me was correct and this is more important than appeasing someone and giving them false hope."

While I had represented some clients in the film industry such as Universal Studios, Steven Spielberg's Amblin Entertainment and George Lucas's Lucas Films, I had never handled a matter involving an adult, X-rated film. But since I had lots of experience successfully pursuing counterfeiters in a wide variety of industries, I guess it was natural for The Mitchell Brothers of San Francisco, producers of the Marilyn Chambers (the original Ivory Snow girl) "classic", "Behind The Green Door", to turn to me for help when their film was being widely counterfeited.

In this new era of Internet porn, I was shocked to hear that anyone was still buying an X-rated movie made in 1972, much less bothering to counterfeit it. I was soon educated by those in the trenches of this unique and interesting industry. Seems that in the pantheon of porn, there are four "classic" films – "Deep Throat" (1972), "Behind The Green Door" (1972), "Debbie Does Dallas" (1978) and "The Devil In Miss Jones" (1973), all which still sell (and are counterfeited) briskly.

After several filings and an equal number of embarrassed Federal Judges, I made the world safe for the "classic" film "Behind The Green Door" and, of course, also the inevitable "Behind The Green Door – The Sequel" (1986). My mother was so proud.

The adult industry also includes the manufacture, distribution, advertising and sale of a wide variety of devices and substances, many of which require/invite intellectual property protection, whether patent, copyright, trademark, trade dress and/or trade secret. And I have had cases involving all. Many such items, previously available only at the likes of Doc Johnson's, now appear on the shelves of your neighborhood RiteAid, albeit discretely near the pharmacist. Some are even advertised on network TV in highly suggestive ads. We have come so far.

A client once invited me to a "trade show" at his enormous warehouse in a God-forsaken, urban wasteland of a former industrial neighborhood. I thought I had seen it all. Turns out I had no clue. I still cannot conceive of (and do not want to think about) what one does with/to most of what I had seen.

And I met many actual porn "stars." Let's just say that sometimes you do not really want what you think you do. Sometimes it is better that a fantasy remain a fantasy.

My legal skills were not always utilized on behalf of adult businesses, sometimes against them. While the Philadelphia Police regularly arrest street walkers, inexplicably. The City Paper and The Philadelphia Weekly include page after page of ads for prostitutes and "massage parlors."

A few years ago, I read in one of those papers that legendary cellist Yo Yo Ma was to appear the next day at the Academy of Music. A few pages later, there was an ad, with a picture of a comely, scantily-clad young Asian lady, for the "Yo Yo Ma Spa."

Since Mr. Ma earns a rather handsome living teasing angelic notes from the depths of his 1712 Stradivarius, I thought it unlikely that he had branched out into massage parlors or that he had licensed his name to these "masseuses." So, on the evening he appeared at The Academy, I had a letter hand delivered to him alerting him to what appeared to be an unauthorized use of his famous name.

Sure enough, the next issue of that urban paper included no further ad for the "Yo Yo Ma Spa" and shortly thereafter, I received a letter of thanks from Mr. Ma's management who obviously had taken measures to stop the illegal use of his name.

One of the fun aspects of IP law is that it presents frequent opportunities to seek or defend against motions for preliminary injunctions. There is nothing like the exhilaration of basically preparing for and trying a case in just a few weeks or sometimes days. Most fun you can have with your clothes on! Often times, the injunction card is played as a clever gambit to force resolution of an otherwise vanilla commercial dispute by getting the matter before a judge quickly and ahead of all others. Such as it was for my licensee client in a seemingly mundane licensing dispute over royalty payments and scope of use under a license. What made it unusual was that the license was for the sale of "reproductions" of male porn stars' "equipment."

The licensor sued for copyright infringement claiming it owned copyright rights in and to each of these "works of art" and had even registered them with the Copyright Office. Well, as criminal defense lawyers say that prosecutors can get a grand jury to indict a ham sandwich, IP lawyers know that lots of things that are not copyrightable get through the Copyright Office.

I had learned in 1978 from Professor Paul Bender at Penn Law School that in order to be copyrightable, a work had to be "an original work of authorship" and it could not be functional. So, I argued that these "works" were merely slavish copies/castings of human body parts and thus, not original. And, that if they had any "author", it was either God or the actors' parents, not the Licensor. Further, these items were clearly "functional" as used for sexual gratification, not works of art.

My opponent, a rather stylish gent, bearing a large gym bag filled with "Exhibits", creatively and amazingly, with a straight face, argued that his client's "works" were indeed "works of art" as they constituted "an homage to the male phallus" – a phrase I never imagined I would hear, must less in a Federal courtroom. As titters rolled through the courtroom filled with observers from a local college, I thought of the scene from Stanley Kubrick's "A Clockwork Orange" wherein Malcolm MacDowell assaults a homeowner with a huge white sculpture, more arguably such an "homage."

The Judge was less amused or distracted. She was a middle-aged, African-American woman had once been an Oakland, CA police officer so I figured she had seen everything. Nonplussed, she asked my foppish opponent to bring forth his "Exhibits" so she could examine these "works of art" for herself. As he eagerly delivered several packaged items to the bench of this Article III Jurist, I stood by quietly knowing my work here was done. A good lawyer knows when to stand down.

The Judge closely examined several "Exhibits" paying particular attention to the "Instructions" on the packaging. She turned to counsel and inquired as to why a work of art had "instructions" and was "dishwasher safe." The licensor's counsel reluctantly acknowledged that his art "homage" could also be used for other purposes. Case closed. Motion denied. ConWest Resources, Inc. v. Playtime Novelties, Inc., 2006 WL 3346226, 2006 U.S. Dist. LEXIS 85461, 84 U.S.P.Q. 2d 1019 (N.D. CA. 11/17/06) - a reported case which copyright law legend William Patry observed "should immediately make its way into copyright casebooks."

Media reports say that Viagra® is the nation's #1 recreational drug. Thus, it is no surprise that enterprising businessmen would seek to counterfeit it and/or replicate its effects using a non-drug dietary supplement, not subject to the rigors of the FDA drug approval process. I recently encountered the latter in a preliminary injunction motion. The owner of a Federally-registered trademark for "STIFF NIGHTS®", for a "male sexual enhancement herbal supplement," one Erb Avore (yes, his real name) sought to stop a couple of my clients from selling product they had purchased in the marketplace claiming it was counterfeit.

As these things are wont to occur, the hefty filings were dumped on me by my clients about 48 hours before the Preliminary Injunction Hearing. Scrambling to investigate the facts and law, we found that plaintiff had not sold any product in two years because his supplier was under indictment for allegedly including an analogue of the active ingredient in Viagra® in his product and the plaintiff's principal was an indicted Co-Conspirator. And, it turned out the papers filed included little, if any, evidence of wrong doing on the part of my clients.

So, I first demanded that plaintiff produce the affiant to testify live and be cross-examined at the hearing. And I contacted the U.S. Attorney handling the case who was very interested to know that a man he was still investigating might be testifying and being crossed in court in a civil case on the very topics pertinent to his investigation. Needless to say, the affiant did not show, plaintiff could not prove its case and the motion was denied. More than one way to skin a cat. Or make the world safe for STIFF NIGHTS.

Comment 5 to Section 1.2 of the Pennsylvania Rules of Professional Responsibility provides that, "Legal representation should not be denied to people who are unable to afford legal services, or whose cause is controversial or the subject of popular disapproval. By the same token, representing a client does not constitute approval of the client's view or activities." As I like to say, everyone is entitled to Intellectual Property protection.

While some may not approve of the adult industry, it is, like all other industries, including cigarettes, guns, and alcohol, entitled to Intellectual Property protection.

"THE 'SECRET' TO LAW SCHOOL SUCCESS"[14]

My nephew, Madison Jared Tillery, graduated from L.S.U. and just matriculated at Loyola Law School in New Orleans. As the only member of my family who did <u>not</u> attend L.S.U., I am viewed as "The Yankee." Amongst other quaint monikers. Despite the plethora of Louisiana lawyers in the family, brother Scott called upon me to give advice to his son about how to succeed in law school.

The request brought back a flood of memories, both pleasant and less so, my favorite of which was stepping out into the 1979 summer sunshine after the bar exam and rejoicing at the fact that never again in my life would someone hand me a little blue book and require that I answer their questions therein in a limited time period. Free at last!

Unfortunately, brother Scott did not ask my advice about whether his son should attend law school. That is a whole other story. I will note, however, what I always tell young bar aspirants who so inquire, "There are far too many lawyers in this country, but still not enough good ones."

The first fully ABA-accredited law school to close, Whitter Law School, did so this year. Indiana Tech Law School had only provisional accreditation, but it, too, just closed. Others have had to merge or close campuses. Law school applications are down 2%, but U.S. law schools still deliver about 37,000 freshly minted bar applicants each year. And competition for good, well-paying legal jobs is fierce.

As we all know, unless you join Daddy's firm (brother Scott did and nephew Matt might in three years), law school grades are the single most important determining factor in the initial job search. With so much at stake and with over 1.3 million

---

[14] The Philadelphia Lawyer, Vol. 80, No. 4, Winter 2017 and LaSalle University St. Thomas More Pre-law Program Website.

members of the bar who went through the ordeal, one would think there would be one work which clearly and succinctly divulged the secrets of success in law school. <u>Law School For Dummies</u>, perhaps? Actually, turns out that one does exist. But it is more a 'how to practice law without a license' primer, <u>not</u> what we seek.

To advise Matt properly, instead of relying on fading memories alone, I went in search of this 'Holy Grail.' Google and Amazon provided a plethora of books, articles and blogs purporting to deliver the goods. Dean Gregory N. Mandel of Temple Law, Dean John Cannon of Drexel Law, and Director of Academic Support, Jessica Pollock Simon and Reference Librarian Robert Hegadorn of Penn Law kindly provided some excellent suggestions. I could leisurely review many sources as I knew I would not, thankfully, have to run that three-year gauntlet again.

Unsurprisingly, many works do <u>not</u> provide what they promise, but rather ramble on in mind-numbing blather of the goals of "thinking like a lawyer" and writing uninteresting, pedantic prose.

There is much written, mostly by law school academics and law review nerds, about how there are no such secrets and one must read and brief all assigned cases, read all the footnotes, and scour all the law review articles to become a baron of the bar. Perhaps they knew the secrets, succeeded because they did and thus, now, jealously guard them to make everyone else suffer and to maintain their own elite status. Just a theory.

ATTENDING CLASS

There is debate about whether law school really needs to be three years or even two. One of this nation's greatest trial lawyers, Patrick Henry, studied law, on his own, for only six weeks before being admitted to the bar. Well, that was 1760.

Some law schools and some professors count attendance and class participation as part of the course grade. Most do not. To this day it galls me that one of my Penn Law classmates, who coincidentally, is now a good friend and one of my partners, attended only the first and last class of our Evidence course, yet he received the highest grade. Yes, of course, he is brilliant and today is viewed by the bar, rightfully so, as a "lawyer's lawyer," but the point should be well-taken. As a good trial lawyer does in thinking about his/her closing from the moment engaged, my colleague focused not on clever Socratic exchanges with our famous professor, but on preparing to ace the exam. Truth be told, I, too, eventually made A's and attended few classes in my third year, instead working full-time at a local firm. Had I received those third year grades in first year, I might have joined my colleague on Law Review and forever have been known as a Blue Book Nerd.

If only someone had told me the secret. Oddly, I had lawyers aplenty in my family – my father, uncle, aunt, great-uncle, and brother. Why did not they impart the wisdom of their experience to me? Probably the same unstated and inexplicable reason I have not to any other. Until now.

Professor Michael C. Dorf of Cornell Law School said it succinctly, "…all or most of your grade will be based on your performance on a final examination. [But.] We do not prepare you to take exams." And this is our introduction to a system of reason, evidence, fairness and justice?

Law school professors may cringe at the following and deny its truth. But they created and perpetuate this system. Magicians are never pleased when someone reveals the truth behind their illusions.

LEGAL WRITING

Not only do law schools not teach how to write an excellent exam answer, they actually teach how to write in a different way. Legal writing courses focus on how to write memoranda on issues presented for a more senior lawyer and briefs for courts. While the former can bear some resemblance to a good exam answer, they are not the same and the latter is anything but.

So, why the big secret? Sure, you may say it is no secret and everyone knows it. I have seen no studies or surveys, but my own experience, coupled with many years of accumulated anecdotal evidence, makes me believe otherwise. And if it is no secret, why do not law schools teach at least a mini-course on how to take an exam? Perhaps entrepreneurial third years with time on their hands should offer tutorials. Or create an app for that. At least one commercial enterprise has been teaching how since 1987, sadly, 11 years too late for me.

FIRST IMPRESSIONS REALLY ARE EVERYTHING

The LSAT may have been the most important exam you ever took up to that point. In large part, it determined what law school you would attend, which, in large part, determined your career opportunities. But your first year (or "1L") exams are even more important. They determine law review membership and class rank, which are often either all access passes or blackballs in the second year interview season for summer associate positions. Which is likely to determine where you begin your practice after graduation and the bar exam.

IT'S THE EXAM, STUPID – DO'S AND DON'TS

My review of law school success "secrets" from many sources can be distilled into a few "Do's" and "Don'ts."

Don't buy casebooks. Don't read the cases. Don't join a study group. Don't attend class. Don't make outlines. Don't participate in class. Don't learn as you did in college. Don't be concerned with policy.

Do type fast. Do buy hornbooks. Do buy most recent bar review books. Do secure prior exams and sample answers. Do take practice exams. Do focus on black letter law. Do "issue spot."

DON'T BE A FOOL

Otto von Bismarck, The Iron Chancellor who almost single-handedly formed modern Germany, famously said, "Fools learn by experience. Wise men learn by the experience of others."

Years ago while teaching a GRE/LSAT prep course, I learned that the single best way to improve one's score was to take practice exams, in real time, and afterwards compare any incorrect answer with the correct ones. That allowed one to learn to think like the test authors. Although not entirely transferable, because one is multiple-choice and the other essay, this post-exam analysis is applicable to law school exams. By reviewing recent exam questions and grade "A" answers, one can understand the link between the factual triggers in the question and the best answers. Like a Porsche, there is no substitute.

HOW TO ANSWER A LAW SCHOOL EXAM QUESTION

Well, this is it. The real secret. Despite how simple it is, most writings in this area do not actually disclose it. And, if they do, it is buried in thousands of words about "thinking like a lawyer." To paraphrase a fellow Louisianan, James Carville, "It's the issue spotting, stupid."

First, there are no right answers. This is not a math or science test. But, you can get the issue or legal rule wrong, so if you raise it, do so properly.

Second, generally, more is better. Quality is important, but quantity is likely to improve your grade. Learn to type as fast as you think, if not faster. And by all means, type. Do not handwrite.

Third, this is not a history, philosophy or political science exam. It is not the time to discuss the policy pros and cons of any legal rule; it is time to identify it, explain how it applies to the fact pattern, and discuss other rules that may be used to get around it.

Fourth, there are at least two sides (or more) to every issue. State them and more. Then think of more.

Fifth, points are given for creativity but stray from the fundamentals only if you have covered them all first.

Sixth, "IRAC." No, not that hapless, fractured nation we illegally invaded in 2003, losing 4,486 troops, costing over $2 trillion, and where we remain at war after 13 years. IRAC is an acronym for the classic law school/bar exam methodology for legal analysis – Issue - Rule – Application - Conclusion. Oddly, there are at least 22 variations of IRAC, including curiously, AFGAN and KUWAIT.

This four-step process, however, is somewhat deceptive. Keep in mind that in a well-conceived law school exam question, every word is a clue, a door for you to open to a plethora of issues, secondary and tertiary. All you have to do is break down every sentence and use each word, phrase, and concept as a springboard to "spot" or identify issues, state rules that apply or could apply, apply them, and reach conclusions – the more, the better. It really is not that difficult. Once you know the secret.

By the way, to paraphrase Professor Dorf, none of this advice, even if followed, will make you a great or even a good lawyer, it will only help you to succeed in law school.

EXPENSIVE IRONY

Now you have it. If you are reasonably bright and do the work, you will do well. The ultimate irony of law school, however, is that after spending three years and scores of thousands on tuition and books, you have to spend another $3500 and take another six week course to learn what you need to know to pass the bar exam.

Neither law school nor life is fair.

Select Recommended Readings

Fischl and Paul, Getting To Maybe: How To Excel On Law School Exams (Carolina Academic Press 1999)

Fredman and Goldberg, Open Book, Succeeding on Exams From The First Day of Law School (Wolters Kluwer 2011)

Ken DeLeon, Success in Law School – a Unique Perspective (top-law-schools.com/success-in-law-schools.com/success-in-law-school.html)

"FAMOUS MONSTERS IN FILM, TV, MAGAZINES AND THE COURTROOM"[15]

Hugh Hefner and Basil Gogos passed away in September within a fortnight of each other. All know the former, legendary founder of <u>PLAYBOY</u>, but fewer know the latter, the finest movie monster artist of all time. And, yes, the two are connected.

Philadelphia is a city of many American firsts – hospital, public library, zoo, university, etc. but who knew that it is also the site of the publication of the first movie monster magazine and the first monster movie TV show with a "horror host"?

Come back with me now to 1957, the year of Sputnik, the Frisbee, American Bandstand and... monsters.

<u>IN FILM</u>

Early that year, some unheralded bean counter at Universal Studios searching for ways to boost revenue and take advantage of the booming new medium of television looked to the studio's vast archive of movies going back to 1912. Although possessing films of all genres, Universal was particularly known for its classic horror movies - 153 in all by then - from "The Phantom Melody" (1920) to "The Monolith Monsters" (1957). Universal hit upon the brilliant idea to package 52 of the their pre-1948 horror films, to be collectively known as "Shock Theatre," for license to local TV stations throughout the country.

<u>ON TV</u>

On October 7, 1957 (my 3rd birthday – according to my older brother, I was already a "little monster"), Philadelphia TV station WCAU debuted its "Shock Theatre" with another Philadelphia first – a horror host – John Zacherle as "ROLAND,"

---

[15] <u>The Philadelphia Lawyer</u>, Vol. 81, No. 1, Spring 2018

a/k/a Zacherly, The Cool Ghoul, a scientist/undertaker, with "IGOR," his lab assistant, and his unseen wife who slept in a coffin. A Penn grad with a flair for the dramatic, the absurd and the gory, Zacherle camped it up between the horror movies and commercials for 92 episodes before taking his show to New York. "Roland" was the first of some 337 such horror hosts who would terrorize the airwaves for the next 60 years – including 68 "Vampires," 53 "Doctors," 25 "Counts," and 8 "Professors," but, curiously, not one lawyer. Perhaps portraying a lawyer as a 'bloodsucker' would be cutting too close to the bone.

Virtually every TV market had its own wacky version. In my hometown of New Orleans, it was Dr. Morgus the Magnificent (Sid Noel) and his black-hooded assistant, Chopsley. The latter was silently played by a 6'7" local motorcycle police officer who happened to be a client of my father. One day my dad brought me to meet Officer Tommy "Chopsley" George. I was terrified until I realized he was not a monster at all.

IN MAGAZINES

Philadelphia "monster" firsts began, but did not end with Roland and Igor. An enterprising 27-year-old Philadelphia artist, Jim Warren (Taubman), inspired by the success of Hefner's PLAYBOY, launched his own "men's" magazine, AFTER HOURS, in early 1957. Though quite tame by today's standards, it landed him in a Philadelphia jail on obscenity charges and the magazine folded after only four issues.

But Warren learned how to produce and distribute a national magazine. If he could not sell sex, he would sell monsters. And he did – FAMOUS MONSTERS OF FILMLAND magazine debuted in February 1958. Publisher Warren and editor Forrest J. Ackerman were amongst the first visionaries to see the enormous potential market for a magazine and ancillary products based on the new Universal television horror movie craze. Born in the peak Baby Boomer year, it somehow fascinated pre-pubescent and teenage males. As with MAD MAGAZINE and The Three Stooges, girls showed no interest, as they either did not appreciate or were just smarter than the boys.

As any magazine publisher from Hefner to Helen Gurley Brown knew, attractive covers sell magazines. Warren knew that still photos from these old black and white horror films would not catch the eye of hyperactive pre-teens on drugstore magazine racks, especially with the colorful competition of a slew of comic books. He needed an artist who could bring "life" to these celluloid monsters in vivid, stark, ghoulish colors.

Basil Gogos was his man. Of Greek heritage, born in Egypt, he came here at 16 to study art. While on his way to a promising career as an illustrator and commercial artist, he got a fateful late night call from Philadelphia. Perhaps drawing upon study of DaVinci's "grotesques", his first FAMOUS MONSTER cover, Vincent Price as Roderick in "The House of Usher" (FMF #9) in November 1960, set the standard, and he later supplied another 50 covers, more than any other artist.

IN MODELS

Entrepreneurs inevitably cashed in on monster madness in music ("The Monster Mash"), TV ("The Addams Family" and "The Munsters") and especially in plastic models. Every pre-teen and teen boy of that era built model cars, airplanes and ships. So it was a natural fit for model company Aurora Plastics Corporation to launch a line of classic monster models – 13 in all, from Frankenstein (1960) to Forgotten Prisoner (1966). I built them all and had them lined up in a 'Monster Hall of Fame' on my bedroom bookcase, right near my "Visible V-8."

As the monster consumer base aged, clever marketers helped them transition from monsters to muscle cars and the opposite sex. Power and sex were always strong but subtle undercurrents in the horror world. Almost every Universal film of this genre includes at least one very attractive and vulnerable young woman and some extraordinary power, man-made or supernatural. And Warren cleverly used both as themes throughout all 191 issues of his FAMOUS MONSTERS magazine (1958-1983). He reached the apex (or nadir) of this combination with the publication in 1969 of VAMPIRELLA magazine – tales of a sexy, powerful, scantily-clad female vampire.

Through it had a good and long run, the monster craze faded by the end of the '60's as its adherents soon faced the real horrors of war overseas in Vietnam and battles at home for civil rights. The intellectual property rights, copyright and trademark, upon which the success of all those films, magazines, and other goods were based, however, had a much longer life. And, like Dracula rising from his coffin, some of them came to life again in a Philadelphia federal courtroom forty years later.

AND IN COURT

Sometimes those whose success is based upon the exclusive rights provided by intellectual property law overreach in enforcement of their rights. So it was with Jim Warren and his FAMOUS MONSTERS OF FILMLAND.

In 2006, Vanguard Productions published a colorful 160-page career retrospective and biography of Basil Gogos entitled Famous Monster Movie Art of Basil Gogos, which included text and 160 reprints of Gogos' artwork, 24 of which had first appeared as covers of issues of Warren's FAMOUS MONSTERS OF FILMLAND, CREEPY or EERIE magazines. Vanguard had Gogos' permission to so publish, but not Warren's. Warren claimed ownership of the copyrights to the 24 works, and he filed suit for copyright infringement in the United States District Court for the Eastern District of Pennsylvania.

Fortunately, Vanguard had insurance coverage and a policy provision that allowed it to select counsel. Vanguard insisted that the insurance company retain me, rather than its regular stable of defense lawyers, due to the complexity of the esoteric copyright and trademark issues at hand.

Not only did I get to handle this fascinating case, I got to meet and depose Jim Warren and Basil Gogos, two pioneers who enriched my childhood immensely with their creations. And, even better, I had the honor of doing battle with one of the giants of the Philadelphia Intellectual Property Bar – the irrepressible Manny D. Pokotilow.

My study of Lincoln as a lawyer (not vampire slayer) taught me to focus only on what he called the "nub" of the case. Thus, for summary judgment purposes, we did not dispute ownership of the Copyrights or that Vanguard had copied all 24 works or that Vanguard had no authorization from Warren to copy. Our defense was simple – Fair Use.

The 1976 Copyright Act, 17 U.S.C. §107, provides that the copying of a copyrighted work is not an infringement where the use is "for purposes such as criticism, comment, news reporting, teaching, scholarship, or research." In determining whether a particular use is Fair Use, courts must consider four factors: (1) the purpose and character of the use, including whether such use is of a commercial nature or is for non-profit educational purposes, (2) the nature of the copyrighted work, (3) the amount and sustainability of the portion used in relation to the copyrighted work as a whole; and (4) the effect of the use upon the potential market for or value of copyrighted work.

After briefing and pun-filled oral argument, Judge Michael Morris Baylson cleverly and judiciously guided the parties through the haunting halls of copyright law in an academic yet entertaining 45-page opinion. Warren v. Spurlock, 645 F. Supp. 2d 402 (E.D. Pa. 2009).

Although we did not know it then, Judge Baylson brought additional relevant talents and interests to the case as a lifelong bibliophile and serious collector of art and art books. In 2015, he and his wife, Dr. Frances Batzer Baylson, donated 30 works of Matisse and several hundred books related to Matisse to the Morgan Library and Museum in New York. He says he has always favored illustrated books, starting with a Bible he received as a child.

This might explain the opening paragraph of his Opinion, in which he referred to monsters throughout history, "From Goliath in the Bible, to Charybdis and Scylla in Homer, to Count Dracula..."

While noting that the Third Circuit had not addressed the issue of whether a court could decide a Fair Use Defense on summary judgment, he found that the Ninth and the Second Circuits, the two which handle the bulk of the nation's copyright cases, both authorize it, and he concluded that he would follow them.

The case included myriad of technical copyright and trademark law issues, such as work-for-hire, copyright ownership, abandonment, use in commerce, trademark ownership by third party, a jus tertii defense, etc., but the "telltale heart" of the case was the Fair Use defense.

The Gogos book was admittedly a commercial use, not for "non-profit educational purposes," but Factor #1 considers whether the accused work is "transformative" of the copyrighted work. Defendants contended the book "is a work of scholarship, comment, and research, and is precisely the type of work that the Fair Use Doctrine is intended to protect." The Court agreed:

> "The book takes the reader through the history of Gogos' work and his career... The book also provides commentary from many respected individuals in the movie monster industry who attest to the quality of the work and his lasting legacy. The Gogos book is a retrospective and an illustrated biography of an artist who was, and remains, important to movie monster enthusiasts."

The Court also found that the copyrighted works were the entire 68-100 page magazines, and therefore Defendants had taken only a small portion (1-1.5%) of each work, and that the covers, while important were not the "heart" of each work, rather the text and still photos inside were.

Finally, the Court found that there was no credible evidence that the Gogos book would in any way diminish the value of Plaintiff's copyrights or adversely affect the market to exploit same, primarily because Mr. Warren had completely failed to exploit his copyrights for 22 years.

Finding all uses were Fair Use, the Court granted summary judgment to Defendants and later awarded them a significant portion of their attorneys' fees.

ALL ROADS …

Somehow all roads lead back to Philadelphia. Just three months after Judge Baylson rendered his Fair Use decision, Philadelphia-based COMCAST Corporation announced it was acquiring controlling interest Universal Studios (and WCAU), including rights to all those monster movies and Philadelphia horror host shows.

POST SCRIPT

A gentlemen and professional in victory or defeat, Manny Pokotilow called to congratulate me and invited me to lunch. Over excellent turtle soup at the Union League, Manny paid me the ultimate compliment, "Kelly, you're the only lawyer in Philadelphia who could have beaten me in this case. Maybe one or two in New York."

Only a real Philadelphia Lawyer would ever say such a thing.

""FOUR MORE BEERS" – ADVENTURES IN ADMIRALTY"

They say you always remember your first. That is, your first big case. Mine may have been more memorable than most.

In such cases, the initial hurdle, of course, is to get the client. For a young lawyer, that is easier said than done. While securing clients is actually very easy, ones who have interesting, substantial cases and can and will pay significant legal fees are scarce and difficult to acquire. Good old fashioned luck and taking advantage of an opportunity play a large part. In that regard, I was both fortunate and took advantage of an opportunity.

In 1980, less than a year after I passed the bar, my apartment building, The Dorchester, on Rittenhouse Square, was purchased by Chicago developer Robert J. Sheridan, who planned to convert it to condominiums and sell all 545 units individually. This was the first major condominium conversion in Philadelphia and the residents were skeptical about this new legal concept of home ownership and especially of the unknown, charming Midwesterner bringing it to town. At the time, Sheridan appeared to be a condo conversion genius, but we were right to be wary as a decade later he filed for bankruptcy, claiming a negative $16.6 million net worth.

At a meeting of panicked residents, I volunteered for the "Legal Committee" to assist it negotiating with the developer. Working closely and intensely for a short time to protect my own and the interests of my neighbors, I got to know another lawyer 16 years my senior who handled litigation in-house for a major oil company.

We negotiated a transition agreement which became the standard in the area for condo conversions and I authored the association's first Rules and Regulations. All pro bono. At some point my new friend said he would like to send me some real, paying work, but could not assign anything significant since I was only a very young and new associate at my firm. I understood, bided my time and was delighted to eventually get a couple small cases.

Not long after, there was a major accident on a ship loading oil at a pipeline depot in Alaska in which able seaman, Harry T. Stewart, not much older than I, lost several fingers and the effective use of his hands. The pipeline depot was owned by a company in which my friend's oil company held controlling interest, so he had say over who would get the representation of the company.

I got the call. My first big case. For my client. I was terrified but let no one know that until this moment.

I grew up in the bustling port city of New Orleans, my cousin was a pilot on the Mississippi, and I often sailed the bayous and lakes of lower Louisiana, so I knew port from starboard, but nothing of admiralty law. However, I was determined to learn, and the deeper I delved into the law of the sea, the more I was intrigued. I considered making it a career and became a Proctor in Admiralty. One of the other defense lawyers later tried to entice me to join his firm, but I demurred, as I had a sense that maritime legal work in this area was not expanding any time soon. Turns out I was right. I have maintained my status as a Proctor these 37 years, but have handled only a handful of admiralty matters since that first.

When I came to the bar, there were only two types of official legal "specialty" universally recognized – members of the Patent Bar enrolled in the U.S. Patent Office and Proctors in Admiralty, seasoned members of the venerable Maritime Law Association of the United States. Today, there are over 1.3 million lawyers in the nation, but only 1,267 Proctors in Admiralty, a bar designation that dates back to the 1200's in England.

There are currently only 49 Proctors in Pennsylvania – about 4% of the total, which might seem appropriate as we have about that percentage of the U.S. population. While Philadelphia was once the largest U.S. port, it is now only 14th.

Like the jaws of the great white whale on Captain Ahab's leg, the Cook Inlet Pipeline oil loader claw clamped down on poor Harry Stewart's powerful, weather beaten hands. The first responders (not actually called that until 9/11) were his fellow seamen, his brothers of the brine. He was evacuated to Anchorage by helicopter within minutes, but sadly suffered serious injuries ending his peripatetic life at sea.

Somehow, probably through referral by his maritime union, as was then as is now often the case, he ended up being represented by a lawyer 4,500 miles away from the scene of the accident – a Philadelphia lawyer, the bombastic and colorful Marvin I. Barish. Fortunately, Marvin seldom appeared in the case, leaving the heavy lifting to his bright, young (though senior to me) colleague, the equally inimitable, Walter Z. Steinman. I do recall vividly one particular amusing performance by Marvin at a deposition when I mused generally about the need for more safety measures in this obviously dangerous work at sea. Marvin leaned over, astonishingly, in the presence of his injured client and said, "You know, I just don't believe in safety." I assumed he was joking, though Walt later told me he probably was not. Twenty years later, Marvin was reprimanded by a local federal judge for screaming obscenities at opposing counsel and threatening to kill him.

Walt became and remains today a good friend and a great plaintiff's personal injury lawyer. He had filed this Jones Act lawsuit in the U.S. District Court for the Eastern District of Pennsylvania because it was a few blocks from his office, the Federal Court in Alaska often requires snowshoes to approach, and Mr. Stewart's employer and ship owner, Keystone Shipping, was based here. As misery loves company, Keystone's lawyer, the witty, but sometimes gruff, E. Alfred Smith, decided to join two other possible sources of remuneration for hapless Harry the seaman, my client-to-be, Cook Inlet Pipeline Company, the terminal operator, and Continental Emsco, the manufacturer of the equipment involved.

Continental Emsco hired Fred Kuffler, then of the storied maritime firm of Palmer, Biezup & Henderson. I soon learned that his firm and that of Al Smith, Krusen, Evans & Byrne, had a serious, but relatively friendly rivalry for maritime defense work in the area. That explained some of the tension and wisecracks in the case which were sometimes as salty as those of the seafarers themselves.

I learned so much from Walt, Al and Fred in that case, but one thing I have never forgotten is the camaraderie and professionalism. Walt actually says it best:

"As I think back, what strikes me most is that it was a much different time for our trial practice. In those bygone days, both sides of the Philadelphia maritime bar mostly got along well and advocated for their clients with civility and cooperation. We traveled together to out-of-state depositions, often staying in the same hotel and having lunch or dinner together after taking hours of testimony. It was nothing to share a rental car or sit together on the flight back to Philly and talk about things other than our case. I don't remember the last time I have done any of that with opposing counsel. And motions to compel discovery were rarely if ever necessary because we knew what was properly shared and we just did it in a fair and honorable way. Also, there was always the respect and understanding that, in the end, this was still a business and we were all just trying to do our best to make a living.

"Boy, have things changed in litigation these days. I may be romanticizing the past a bit, but it seemed back then that it was only the actual issues that mattered, getting to the truth for the benefit of our respective clients rather than all of the cut-throat games and tactics of today which just delays our progress and makes lawsuits unnecessarily expensive. For obvious reasons, I know we have all had to adapt and venture into non-maritime matters for years now and to me the general litigation bar has just never had that same feeling of adversarial camaraderie that we used to have among the admiralty lawyers."

100 MILE BULGE

I had done moderately well in Professor A. Leo Levin's Civil Procedure course at Penn in 1976-77, but somehow missed the seldom invoked 100 Mile Bulge Rule – F.R.Civ.P. 4(k)(1)(B). With all the righteous indignation a young lawyer can muster, I filed a Motion to Dismiss my client for lack of personal jurisdiction as it did business only in Alaska, never in Pennsylvania. Well, I was soon schooled (or re-schooled) in the arcana of civil procedure by Al Smith and his sharp associate Peter H. Bach. Seems that my client was a Delaware corporation, a joined third-party and thus "not more than 100 miles" from the E.D. PA Court which issued the summons and thus, according to this Rule, had personal jurisdiction. Bloodied, but unbowed, I pressed on to the merits, focusing on how to put the blame primarily, if not completely, on the shipping company and the manufacturer.

WHO, WHAT, WHEN, WHERE, HOW AND WHY

As I was to learn on the job, the first thing one has to determine in a maritime accident is how it happened, then why it happened and, finally, who, if anyone, was factually and legally responsible. Although the injured seaman may sometimes bear some responsibility, absent evidence of impairment, reckless behavior, or intentional act, that hatch should remain closed. The operation being conducted involved coordination between Seaman Stewart, his fellow seamen, all employees of defendant Keystone, owner of the ship and co-defendant Cook Inlet Pipeline Company employees utilizing equipment designed and provided by Co-Defendant Continental Emsco.

I was shocked and very concerned that both Keystone's and Continental Emsco's lawyers vociferously denied that their clients were at fault in any way and agreed that only my client was to blame. Until Walt laughed out loud and told me that Al and Fred said this in every case.

Nevertheless, if I were to defend my client with zeal, I knew I would have to find ways to establish the liability, at least shared, of their clients.

DISCOVERY IN THE DARK AGES

In that pre-electronically-stored document era, groups of lawyers gallivanting around the country to review and inspect thousands of paper documents in odd and uncomfortable places was the norm. Paper discovery requests produced actual paper responses.

-161-

My client's documents were housed in a remote, unheated warehouse in Wasilla, Alaska. Sarah Palin, then co-captain and point guard of the Wasilla High School girl's basketball team, was nearby earning her first nickname – "Sarah Barracuda." Not knowing I was missing an encounter with this future Vice-Presidential candidate, I had the 50 or so boxes of documents sent to a company office in Texas for my review and production. As an original Louisianan, I had no love for the Lone Star State. We always said the best thing to come out of Texas was Interstate 10. Though I really prefer Civil War Union General Phil Sheridan's quip, "If I owned Texas and Hell, I would rent out Texas and live in Hell."

Well, for a couple of weeks, I lived in Texas with thousands of dusty, smelly oil company records, and it might as well have been Hell.

Sometimes those long, arduous trips produced gallows humor not quite politically correct. Al Smith was particularly witty, or so he thought, when he insensitively often repeated the joke, "How does Harry Stewart order 4 more beers?" then holding up a hand with only the first and little finger raised.

AND IN THE END …

As do 98.2% of Federal civil cases, this one settled before trial.

An E.D.PA. Federal Judge told me last week that when he came to the bar in 1970, 600 cases a year were tried in our Courthouse. Now, although the dockets have mushroomed, it is only 150.

After months of finger pointing at the other two defendants, each of the three ponied up a third of what we all agreed was a reasonable settlement. It seemed like a King's ransom to me at the time, but, in retrospect, it was not sufficient compensation for the taking of one digit of a young working man's hand, much less seven or eight. It made me question the wisdom of the way we litigate and compensate personal injuries. But, I suppose, until we can regenerate human appendages, this is the best we can do for the Harry T. Stewarts of the world. Not even the 66 declared miracles at Lourdes include regrown limbs or digits. I am sorry, Harry, wherever you are.

"NOT JUST A HANDSHAKE"[16]

When I was in 8th grade, one of my teachers thought it would be an excellent learning experience for the class to conduct a mock trial based upon a fictional murder he elaborately orchestrated on the playground during recess. He thought that because I was the only class member who was the offspring of a lawyer, I might serve well in the role of the Judge. The only actual experience I had had with the law had been that close call in '66 with a Wildlife & Fisheries Agent (we were in Louisiana, after all), so I asked my father if I could attend one of his trials to help prepare for the role.

Though my father was not strictly a trial lawyer, he did a little bit of everything as a general practitioner in suburban New Orleans, including, on occasion, service as pro bono appointed counsel for indigent criminal defendants. To me, he was Atticus Finch, Clarence Darrow, and Abraham Lincoln all rolled into one.

As it happened, he was scheduled to defend a young man in a murder trial, just weeks before my appearance as "Judge Tillery" in the "trial" of State of Ferncrest (my grade school) v. Mark Jefferson Davis (really). Dad patiently explained the basics of a trial as I, wide-eyed, took copious notes about openings, direct and cross-examination, evidence, objections, 5th Amendment, closings, burdens of proof, jury charges, deliberation, and verdict.

Wow! While it was not rocket science, it was a lot to absorb at 13. I was particularly impressed, however, with the fundamental fairness of the system. If that Agent had caught me and Butchy with those 10 under-sized red snapper, I knew that this was the system in which I would have wanted to have been tried.

In any event, for 5 days in a blistering St. Bernard Parish courtroom, I watched my father masterfully defend a man on trial for his life. As it turned out, the prosecution unwisely depended

---

[16] The Philadelphia Lawyer, Vol. 81, No. 2, Summer 2018

entirely on the testimony of two particularly unsavory characters who wilted under cross-examination like snow on a gator's back. The unjustly accused man was freed, Dad was a (and my) hero, and I learned how our justice system worked.

What really struck me, however, was not the trial, but a single moment just after the Judge discharged the defendant. After eviscerating the prosecution with everything from scalpel to chainsaw, my Dad put away his papers, closed his old, tan briefcase, walked slowly over to the beleaguered prosecutor and extended his hand. The prosecutor looked up, smiled and gave my Dad a firm, warm handshake.

I will never forget that moment – my Dad, magnanimous in victory, the prosecutor, humble in defeat, but both professionals – members of an elite and honorable group, dedicated to justice.

For the first time in my life, I thought – now there is a brotherhood I want to join.

That moment came to mind again recently when, twice, my opponent refused to shake my hand after proceedings. In 38 years of litigating in state and federal courts in 40 different states, I cannot recall that ever happening before. Even in New York and Los Angeles. Shamefully, the miscreant is a prominent member of the Philadelphia Bar. I was shocked, disappointed and embarrassed. For him, for his associates then present, for his firm, and for the bar.

So much can be said in one gesture. Or in the absence of one.

Lest you think there was some history between us or that I had said something untoward about his mother that might justify such a snub, I must disappoint. And, if it had happened only once, I might attribute it to his having a bad day and let it pass. But it happened twice. And when you see that same disdainful look in the eyes of a man refusing your proffered hand, twice, you know it is as intentional as it is petty.

We have been shaking hands to show we come in peace since the Greeks did it in the 5th century B.C. Today, it is a sign of trust and respect. Although, curiously, British barristers have a tradition of not shaking hands with their opponents, the "American Rule" is decidedly the opposite. Or at least it has been since colonial times.

As my constitutional law professor and District Court Judge Louis H. Pollak once said, "The litigator need not hug an adversary. But to treat an adversary with advertent discourtesy – let alone with calumny or derision – is a form of incivility that rends the fabric of the law."

The second incident occurred after an appellate argument also attended by a class of Philadelphia school children learning about the majesty of our legal system. Thankfully, the unprofessional and uncivil affront occurred after they had departed for Independence Hall. Their teacher would have found it hard to explain.

By the way, he lost both the motion and the appeal. The Germans call it schadenfreude.

A number of courts, state Bars, and Bar Associations actually have rules about this professional and common courtesy. For example, Section 10 of the Alabama State Bar "Code of Professional Courtesy" provides "When each adversary proceeding ends, a lawyer should shake hands with the fellow lawyer who is the adversary ..." And the San Diego County Bar Association Attorney Code of Conduct, Section III, (O), provides, "Lawyers should conduct themselves so that they may conclude each case with a handshake with the opposing lawyer."

Lest we Philadelphia Lawyers be any less civil or professional than our colleagues at the Bar in such disparate and distant places as Alabama and San Diego, the next time a proceeding ends in which you are counsel, stand up, walk over to opposing counsel, and extend your hand.

We are, after all, professionals.

V. THE COURTS

"THE TOP TEN WORST U.S. SUPREME COURT DECISIONS"[17]

On April 9, 2010, just eleven days before his 90th birthday, Supreme Court Justice John Paul Stevens gave notice of his retirement which will allow President Obama to appoint a second Supreme Court Justice less than two years into his first term. The nominee, Solicitor General Elena Kagan, is destined to be compelled to endure lengthy, probing and sometimes inane examination in Senate confirmation hearings. Since nominees are often asked about past Supreme Court decisions and, if confirmed, will be asked to wrestle with monumental legal issues, perhaps an examination of how previous Supreme Court Justices sometimes got it so wrong and did so much damage might be valuable for all.

Only 111 human beings have served on the nation's highest court since its creation on September 24, 1789 by the first Judiciary Act. One-hundred nine (98%) of those unelected jurists have been white, only two African-American. All men (97%), except three women. All Christian (93.6%), except seven Jews.

From its first case, the uneventful and purely procedural West v. Barnes, 2 U.S. 401 (1791), to its most recent providing First Amendment protection for "crush videos" (if you have to ask, you do not want to know), United States v. Stevens, 08-769 (4/2/2010), the Court has issued almost 25,000 Opinions. Of those, some are very brief, others quite lengthy, some are erudite, others are crude, some are mundane and others are awe-inspiring. And some are really, really bad. Not just in style or language, but in principle, holding and, most importantly, in the effect on millions of lives.

---

[17] The Philadelphia Lawyer, Vol. 73, No. 2, Summer 2010, and reprinted in Jewish Social Policy Network Newsletter, August 2010 and in Law For The Business Enterprise, Samuel D. Hodge, Jr. (2d Ed. Learning Solutions, 2012) and in Legal and Regulatory Environment For Business, Samuel D. Hodge, Jr. (McGraw Hill 2014)

While there is disagreement based mostly on extremes in ideology and/or religious belief, there appears to be legal and historical scholarly consensus on a number of opinions that are the "worst." Since there are more than ten, honing the list down to the "Top Ten" is not easy or simple, but I have tried, acknowledging that others may disagree with one or more being included or feel I have omitted one or more of their "favorites."

I have tried to include those cases which (a) dealt with fundamental issues important to society as a whole, (b) had a profound effect on a large number of people for a long time and (c) were ultimately overruled and/or rendered a nullity by subsequent decision, legislation, Constitutional Amendment and/or common consensus. Thus, the list cannot include decisions that were just dumb, like FCC. v. Pacifica Foundation, 438 U.S. 726 (1978) [upholding ban on broadcast of George Carlin's famous "seven words you can't say on radio"], or highly controversial ones like Bush v. Gore, 531 U.S. 98 (2000) [2000 Presidential Election], Roe v. Wade, 410 U.S. 113 (1973) [legalization of abortion] or Kelo v. City of New London 545 U.S. 469 (2005) [eminent domain taking for private developer]. After selection based upon these criteria of my own design, I discovered, somewhat to my surprise, an interesting and disturbing common theme. Each one, as shall be seen, involved the shameful, disdainful treatment by the powerful of minorities and their rights. And in each, the Court sided with the powerful, consigning the minority often to generations of abuse and/or denial of fundamental rights. In each, unbiased observers agree that the decisions adversely impacted millions for several and sometimes many generations.

Only one was a 5-4 decision. Four were unanimous. Seven deal with laws of the states of the Deep South. All, but one, were decided by all white men over 50 years of age. Some majority opinions were by legendary justices, such as Oliver Wendell Holmes, Jr., some by racist ideologues such as Roger B. Taney, and some by rightfully unheralded journeymen such as George Sutherland. Size did not seem to matter. Dred Scott produced the longest opinions at 234 pages and Pace the shortest at two.

While the majorities in each case seemed tone deaf to the fundamental wrongheadedness of their decisions, at the time of each there was always a small, but often vocal, minority of individuals, lawyers, academics and organizations who recognized that the Court had done the wrong thing and would inevitably end up on the wrong side of history. Sometimes vindication took as little as a few years, sometimes almost a century.

A review of this list may also inform and enlighten as to where the Court is going and/or should go on such timely and difficult issues as same-sex marriage, Perry v. Schwarzenegger, N.D.CA., cv-09-2292, or Arizona's "Papers, please." immigration law, which are likely to land on the Court's docket in the not-so-distant future.

And the "winners," in chronological order, are:

1.   Dred Scott v. Sandford, 60 U.S. 393 (1857) [actually, "Sanford", but a clerk's error altered this infamous slave owner's name]

> Majority Opinion: Chief Justice Roger B. Taney
> Vote: 7 to 2 (Justices John McLean and Benjamin R. Curtis Dissenting)
> Overruled By: 14th Amendment, Section 1 (1868)

This is, of course, the "Mother of All Bad Supreme Court Decisions." Even the most rabid "strict constructionist" and the most bleeding heart liberal will readily agree that this one merits inclusion.

The Court, per octogenarian Chief Justice Taney (pronounced "Tawney"), the original "originalist," held that Mr. Dred Scott was a slave and not a citizen of the United States as that word is used in the Constitution, and thus had no standing to sue his owner in a federal court for his freedom and/or for the freedom of his wife, Harriet, and their children, Eliza (14) and Lizzie (7). In twenty thousand words of tortured logic and faulty legal history, Tancy condemned an entire family to servitude because the Court found it had no jurisdiction.

I have read a great deal about slavery in America, from Harriet Beecher Stowe's iconic Uncle Tom's Cabin (1852) to Kenneth M. Stampp's classic The Peculiar Institution (1956), but I have never felt the chill of governmental indifference to the then 4 million plus human beings in bondage until I read this opinion of our highest court as it so blithely turned the freedom of a man and his family into a matter of civil procedure.

2.   United States v. Cruikshank, 92 U.S. 542 (1875)

> Majority Opinion: Chief Justice
> Morrison R. Waite
> Vote: 8 to 1 (Justice Nathan Clifford
> Dissenting)
>
> The Civil Rights Cases, 109 U.S. 3 (1883)
>
> Majority Opinion: Justice Joseph P.
> Bradley
> Vote: 8 to 1 (Justice John M. Harlan
> Dissenting)
> Overruled By: Civil Rights Act of
> 1964 – Upheld in Heart of Atlanta
> Motel, Inc. v. U.S., 379 U.S. 241
> (1964)

Although separated by seven years, these two related cases share a spot since they concern, respectively, the criminal and civil abandonment by the Court of negro citizens in the South to Jim Crow and the KKK for almost a century. In Cruikshank, a case arising from the Colfax Massacre of 1873 when almost 100 negro men were murdered by an organized group of white men in Louisiana, the Court held that the U.S. could not charge the accused with violations of the Civil Rights' Enforcement Act of 1870 ("The Ku Klux Klan Act"). In one fell swoop, the Court effectively emasculated all efforts of the U.S. to use Federal criminal law to restrain the abuses of the KKK and similar groups throughout the South. A hundred years of lynchings, murder, abuse and mayhem would follow.

Likewise, in The Civil Rights Cases, the Court via Justice Bradley (former railroad lawyer, already infamous for being the deciding vote that made Rutherford B. Hayes President in the "Stolen Election of 1876" – yes, there was one before 2000), struck down as unconstitutional the Civil Rights Act of 1875, which was enacted to ensure equal access for all, no matter what their race or color, to "inns, public conveyances on land or water, theatres and other places of public amusement." In dissent, Justice John Marshall Harlan opined that the Acts were well within the power of Congress, including under the Commerce Clause.

Almost a century later, the Court would uphold a similar Civil Rights Act in Heart of Atlanta Motel, utilizing much of the reasoning of "The Great Dissenter."

3.   Pace v. Alabama, 106 U.S. 583 (1883)

> Majority Opinion: Justice Stephen Field
> Vote: Unanimous
> Overruled By: Loving v. Virginia, 388 U.S. 1 (1967)

The heartless Court, in a barren two-page decision, upheld the convictions of Tony Pace, a negro man and Mary T. Cox, a white woman, who had been found guilty of violation of an Alabama law which prohibited marriage, adultery or fornication between "any negro" and "any white person." Each had been sentenced to two years in the state penitentiary. Justice Field, in a clever feat of legal legerdemain, held that the statute did not violate the 14th Amendment Equal Protection Clause because it, in fact, treated whites and negroes equally — both races were prohibited from marrying, cheating with, and fornicating with the other.

Eighty years later, the Warren Court would disagree in the aptly-named Loving v. Virginia, establishing not only that laws against interracial marriage are unconstitutional, but that Virginia really is for lovers.

4.   Plessy v. Ferguson, 163 U.S. 537 (1896)

> Majority Opinion: Justice Henry B. Brown
> Vote: 7 to 1 (Justice John M. Harlan Dissenting)
> Overruled By: Brown v. Board of Education, 347 U.S. 483 (1954)

        Though known for little else, former Detroit corporate lawyer Justice Henry Billings Brown bequeathed to generations of Americans the insidious "legal" concept of "separate but equal." The Court held that enforcement of a Louisiana statute that required railway companies to provide and police "equal, but separate accommodations for the white and colored races" did not violate either the 13th or 14th Amendment. Homer Plessy had challenged racial separation in public transportation 63 years before Rosa Parks. Justice Harlan, in a brilliant and bitter dissent, stated presciently, "In my opinion the judgment this day rendered will, in time, prove to be quite as pernicious as the decision made by this tribunal in the Dred Scott case." It would take 58 years, the eloquence of NAACP Counsel Thurgood Marshall and the political skills of Chief Justice Earl Warren for the Court to overrule this vile concept unanimously.

5.   Cumming v. Richmond County Board of Education, 175 U.S. 528 (1899)

> Majority Opinion: Justice John M. Harlan
> Vote: Unanimous

> Lum v. Rice, 275 U.S. 78 (1927)

> Majority Opinion: Chief Justice William H. Taft
> Vote: Unanimous

        Though separated by 28 years, these two gems deserve joint scorn as they both evidence the Court's insensitivity to race and equality in public education. In Cumming, Justice Harlan, surprisingly, opined for the Court that Georgia's failure to provide a high school for "colored" children as it did for white children did not violate the 14th Amendment, while in Lum the Court held that Mississippi's refusal to permit a child of Chinese descent to attend the "white," school in her district, rather than a "colored" school in a neighboring district because she was not "white" was constitutionally permissible. The Court did everything but sanction a Pantone® Chart test for entitlement to educational benefits.

While no case specifically overruled either, Brown v. Board of Education effectively negated each.

6.   Lone Wolf v. Hitchcock, 187 U.S. 553 (1903)

> Majority Opinion: Justice Edward D. White
> Vote: Unanimous
> Overruled By: Delaware Tribal Business Comm. v. Weeks, 430 U.S. 73 (1977)

Justice White, in fewer than six pages, cavalierly dismissed the entire history of the indigenous peoples of America and, more particularly, all of the agreements made with them by the United States, holding that they exist in a "relation of dependency" "towards the government," that is, "wards of the nation," and thus the Congress has "paramount power" over Indian lands. The Court held that the Fifth Amendment did not protect interest in Indian lands and the Federal Government could pretty much do what it wanted with them. And, of course, it did, abrogating treaties, ignoring promises and agreements for generations, treating the Indian as badly as, if not worse than, Jim Crow treated the negro.

7.   Buck v. Bell, 274 U.S. 200 (1927)

> Majority Opinion: Justice Oliver Wendell Holmes, Jr.
> Vote: 8 to 1 (Justice Pierce Butler Dissenting)

In 1927, the "eugenics" movement was gaining ground, and not just in Germany. When the State of Virginia engaged the mighty force of the U.S. Supreme Court to prevent Carrie Buck, 18, from ever bearing children again, the venerable Civil War veteran Oliver Wendell Holmes, Jr. obliged. The Court ruled that it was not unconstitutional for a state to determine that it, the unwilling adult victim and presumably her yet to be born children, would be better off if she were forcibly sterilized.

Holmes observed that Ms. Buck, was "feeble minded," as was her mother and her daughter. Though later investigation proved that not to be entirely true, Holmes relied on the trumped-up record to pontificate that, in his infamous observation, "Three generations of imbeciles are enough."

After reading these cases, one might come to agree with Holmes if it applied to certain Supreme Court Justices.

Like some others, Buck was never officially overturned, though no one seriously believes it is still good law.

8.   Ozawa v. United States, 260 U.S. 178 (1922)

        Majority Opinion: Justice George Sutherland
        Vote: Unanimous

        United States v. Thind, 261 U.S. 204 (1923)

        Majority Opinion: Justice George Sutherland
        Vote: Unanimous

Some of the Court's opinions on race are so absurd as to be laughable if they were not so sad and serious in effect. Ozawa and Thind rank together as such. In Ozawa, the Court held that "a person of the Japanese race" is not a "white person" and therefore cannot become a naturalized citizen. In Thind, the Court held similarly for a "high caste Hindu of full Indian blood." More Pantone® testing, courtesy of Justice Sutherland, one of the conservative "Four Horsemen" who held back the progress of the New Deal for years.

9.   Korematsu v. United States, 323 U.S. 214 (1944)

> Majority Opinion: Justice Hugo L. Black
> Vote: 6 – 3 (Justices Owen J. Roberts, Francis W. Murphy and Robert H. Jackson Dissenting)
> "Overruled" By: Korematsu v. United States, U.S.D.Ct., N.D. Cal. (1983)
> Writ of Coram Nobis granted-
> conviction overturned

It is said that "hard cases make bad law." If our current experiences post-9/11 are too close in time and too personal to bring that home, nothing can do it better than Korematsu. Therein, the Court upheld the conviction of an American citizen of Japanese descent (Nisei) for failure to obey an Executive/Military Order to leave his home and evacuate the West Coast solely because he was of Japanese descent. Although the Court was asked to pass "…upon the whole subsequent detention program in both assembly and relocation centers......," in obtuse and cowardly fashion, it refused to do so. However, the Court made its feelings clear that it would give ultimate deference on such matters to the Military and the Executive. That had always worked out so well for protecting rights of minorities in the past.

10.   Bowers v. Hardwick, 478 U.S. 186 (1986)

> Majority Opinion: Justice Byron R. White
> Vote: 5 to 4 (Justice Harry A. Blackmun for the Dissenters)
> Overruled By: Lawrence v. Texas, 539 U.S. 553 (2003)

Only 24 years ago, the Court upheld as constitutional a Georgia statute that criminalized private, non-commercial, adult, consensual sexual activity. Despite the fact that the law applied equally to heterosexual as well as homosexual activity, Justice White focused oddly and only on homosexual activity, apparently fearing, in homophobic paranoia, that any contrary ruling might establish a society-destroying "fundamental right to engage in homosexual sodomy."

Justice Powell cast the deciding vote, although his concurring opinion evidences reluctance to join the majority. Indeed, some years later, he expressed regret about his vote, saying he 'just had just not known any gay people.' In fact, unbeknownst to him, he had, very well. One of his law clerks from only five years before <u>Bowers</u> was gay.

Seventeen years later the Court overruled <u>Bowers</u>, though even then by only a 6 to 3 vote.

PREDICTION

If nothing else, these Top Ten evidence that the Court does sometimes make grievous errors and that it can, at least in time, correct them. As (if) we continue to become a more enlightened society, I predict that we will in the foreseeable future see at least two fundamental societal changes brought on by Supreme Court decisions (1) the legalization of same sex marriage and (2) the elimination of the death penalty. Stay tuned.

"WHEN THEY TELEVISED FEDERAL TRIALS – BACK TO THE FUTURE"[18]

PULLING THE PLUG

On January 13, 2010, the U.S. Supreme Court issued an unprecedented Order stopping the live audio-video streaming of an important District Court Bench Trial. Perry v. Schwarzenegger, N.D.CA. 3:09-cv-02292, 588 U.S. (2010) [No. 09A648]. In that civil rights trial, high-powered lawyers David Boies and Ted Olson sought to (and did) invalidate, as unconstitutional, California's "Proposition 8" which had reversed a State Supreme Court decision permitting same sex marriage. The State refused to defend, leaving that to various self-styled advocacy groups.

Five Justices overruled District Court Chief Judge Vaughn R. Walker (and Ninth Circuit Chief Judge Alex Kozinski), affecting a blackout based on a procedural ruling that a statute was likely violated when a local rule was revised. Although the Court twice cautioned that it would not express "any view on whether such trials should be broadcast", it did precisely that and made its position clear – Federal trials should not be televised. While acknowledging that the issues being tried in this "high profile trial" were "the subject of public debate throughout the state, and indeed, nationwide," it concluded, "This case is therefore not a good one for a pilot program," implying, strangely, that only cases in which there is little public interest would be appropriate for televising. The last time the Court stopped anything like this was the re-counting of Florida votes in Bush v. Gore. Ironically, Ted Olson was Counsel for Bush and David Boies for Gore.

The Prop 8 supporters claimed broadcasting might cause "harassment, economic reprisal, threat and even physical

---

[18] The Philadelphia Lawyer, Vol. 74, No 1, Spring 2011, and reprinted in Oregon State Bar Association Bulletin Magazine, June 2011 and in Lexology (Association of Corporate Counsel)

violence" to their witnesses. A close examination of those claims revealed that they were, as Ted Olson observed, "utterly unsubstantiated and groundless speculation" based solely on claims of paid expert witnesses whose identities and views were already widely-publicized.

Not only is this the first time the Supreme Court ever literally "pulled the plug" on televising a trial, but it was also done in a case which was the "poster child" for televising trials. The only issue at hand was simply live streaming to Courtrooms in five other cities. The case was a civil, non-jury, public dispute involving only already prominent, adult litigants. It was/is history in the making, involving social and constitutional issues affecting millions and certain to land on the Supreme Court's docket. And, it was probably the civil trial attracting more interest than any other in years.

The Court's micromanagement, however, included a provision which exposes the flawed reasoning behind the prohibition. While blindly accepting the baseless protestations of danger, it did not completely prohibit electronic "courtroom expansion," which may be the intellectual seed of the eventual reversal of the ban. Although it prohibited live streaming to courtrooms in other courthouses around the country, it permitted same to other rooms within the same Courthouse. Not even a "Philadelphia Lawyer" could explain a principled distinction between what was prohibited and what was permitted.

NEELY V. CLUB MED – LESSONS FROM THE PAST

This Order brought to mind a simpler time, long ago, when a small window of judicial transparency opened, when a few Federal civil trials were actually televised. And, I tried one of them.

I have long confined my practice to Intellectual Property Law but early in my career handled maritime cases and became a Proctor in Admiralty. While that combination of legal specialties is admittedly unusual, the last maritime case I tried, Neely v. Club Med, was even more so, in several ways, not the least of which was being nationally televised under a Federal Pilot Program.

-182-

In 1993, COURT TV, Steven Brill's then only two-year-old cable channel, televised this 9-day Jury Trial, complete with color commentary and analysis by Doug Llewelyn (originally of "The People's Court") and Jay Monahan (1956-1998) , a New York Trial Lawyer and husband of (then) NBC's Katie Couric.

My client, Eileen Neely, a scuba diving instructor, had been seriously injured in a diving accident on a Club Med expedition in St. Lucia. COURT TV believed the case would be of interest to its viewers and neither Ms. Neely nor I had objection. Club Med, however, strenuously objected, and particularly so to a COURT TV Press Release calling it "a fascinating personal injury case" and "a real tale of horrors."

"HAMSTER OF THE DAY"

Our Trial Judge, the inimitable Robert S. Gawthrop, III (1943-1999), was singularly unimpressed:

> "That is what happens in a free society. ... This is a civil case, not a criminal case, but not a civil case involving the tender psyche of a young child . . .

> * * *

> . . . people have a right to know what is happening in a public forum, which is a United States District Court . . .

> * * *

> . . . other Judges on this Court who have heard trials, apparently things have gone along smoothly. I am supposed to give it a trial run, do the experiment.

You happen to be the hamster of the day."

After hearing 24 witnesses, the Jury returned a verdict for Plaintiff of $556,700.

Club Med appealed, but the Third Circuit, en banc, upheld the verdict. 63 F.3d 166 (1995).

Despite Club Med's initial concerns, there was no evidence that the filming and broadcast had any effect whatsoever on the Judge, any witness, counsel, juror or the outcome. Even Club Med's Trial Counsel now concurs.

One concern is that participants might "perform." That was not our experience. Judge Gawthrop was well known for his performances off the bench, particularly his magnificent baritone voice in Gilbert and Sullivan works, but his "15 minutes of fame" on national camera did not alter his always professional behavior on the bench. While he did pepper the record with bon mots and witticisms, such as, "Maritime Law is difficult to fathom," that was standard fare for this unique jurist, not at all due to the presence of cameras.

PILOT PROJECT

In 1994, the Federal Judicial Conference rejected the recommendation of its own Committee to authorize recording and broadcasting of civil proceedings. Based upon a 3 year Pilot Project, the Committee concluded that, "Most jurors and witnesses believe electronic media presence has no or minimal detrimental effects on witnesses and jurors," and "Judges and attorneys reported observing little or no effect of camera presence on participants in the proceedings, courtroom decorum, on the administration of justice."

Despite the paucity of problems, the Conference somehow "concluded" that "the intimidating effect of cameras on some witnesses and jurors was cause for concern." Oddly, the 28 Conference Judges who regularly make decisions based only upon evidence, not only ignored the compelling evidence supporting their Committee's recommendation, but also failed to explain upon what evidence, if any, they based their contrary "conclusions."

While anecdotal, the real "evidence" from Neely is clear – not one witness or juror was intimidated. The jurors were never filmed. The two stationary cameras were unobtrusive.

In 221 years, Neely was one of only 35 complete Federal civil trials broadcast. In not one of those cases was the filming or broadcast made an issue on appeal. That fact alone is more telling than any fears, concerns or beliefs.

RIGHT TO ATTEND

The Supreme Court has said that "A trial is a public event." Craig v. Harney, 331 U.S. 367 (1947) and held that the right to attend a criminal trial is "implicit in the guarantees of the First Amendment" Richmond Newspapers, Inc. v. Virginia, 448 US 555,580 (1980), while implying that the same holds true for civil trials. Four Circuit Courts have actually held that it does.

Thus, every citizen has a Constitutional "right to attend" every Federal trial. Obviously, it is physically impossible for more than a few hundred to attend any trial. And, truth be told, present courtroom capacity is more than adequate to meet current demand. However, on occasion there is intense and widespread interest in trials occurring far from many who are interested. Perry was such a case.

TRANSPARENCY - VIRTUAL ACCESS

Since 1979 for the House and 1986 for the Senate, gavel-to-gavel television coverage has brought the Legislative Branch into our living rooms. The Judicial Branch, however, remains accessible only by rationing, governed by timing and courtroom location and capacity.

In a world where we can watch live video of a news anchor's colonoscopy or an environmental disaster a mile below the ocean surface, surely we ought to be able to view a few interesting Federal civil trials in the same manner. Without electronic "courtroom expansion," this "right of access" will be a reality only for the rich and the retired. Although the Founding Fathers might not have anticipated this dilemma, or at least its electronic solution, surely they did not intend that result.

LOST TO HISTORY

The technology to televise trials has existed for almost 70 years and the ability to record audio and video has existed for 115 years. In that time, only a handful of the hundreds of significant/interesting Federal civil trials have been recorded and/or broadcast to wider-than-courtroom audiences. How much history have we lost? The few recordings of famous trials that exist are riveting and the few of the not-so-famous are useful teaching tools.

A ROOM TOO SMALL

In 1994, cameras were large, the Internet was in its infancy and You Tube was science fiction. As Guttenberg's Mazarin Bible changed the world in 1453, electronic media technology has revolutionized virtually everything, including access to our courts.

Even if there had been any significant evidence to support the Conference's ban in the past, there is none today. Almost every state court system permits cameras in civil courtrooms, and many have done so for years. There is no chaos in our state courts, at least none attributable to cameras.

Senior Judge Jack B. Weinstein, cogently observed:
"In our democracy, the knowledgeable tend to be more robustly engaged in public issues. Information received by direct observation is often more useful than that strained through the media.

Actually seeing and hearing court proceedings, combined with commentary of informed members of the press and academia, provides a powerful device for monitoring the courts." Hamilton v. Accutek, 942 F. Supp 136, 137-139 (E.D.N.Y. 1996)

"BACK TO THE FUTURE"

Although there is no bill pending in Congress on this issue, such bills have been introduced every year since 1997. While the Obama Administration has not yet formally spoken, considering its stated reverence for "transparency", it might be expected to favor cameras. The Bush Administration, not surprisingly, consistently opposed any electronic media coverage of any Court proceeding. Judge Kozinski, also a member of the Judicial Conference, recently spoke in favor, arguing that 47 states permit it and the Federal Courts must reconsider "in light of current technology." The Supreme Court itself has said that "the time may come" when technology and experience establish that concerns about television coverage are no hazard to a fair trial.

The entire citizenry is entitled to see its judiciary function. A well-informed public which shares and preserves its record of justice will be a better public. The present archaic ban, based on little evidence and unfounded fears, will fall.

NEW PILOT PROGRAM

In fact, there is hope. On September 15, 2010 the Judicial Conference announced a new 3-year Pilot Program to evaluate the effect of cameras in Federal Court rooms.

I expect that when completed in 2013, even those who so fervently opposed cameras in the courtroom, will see, as we did so long ago in Neely, that they do no harm and bring great benefit. Stay tuned.

"COST OF CIVIL JUSTICE"[19]

Every few days I receive an online reports of all civil cases filed in the local federal and state courts. It occurred to me that these reports tell us a lot about our profession, our legal system, and our community. If an alien arrived and had only this evidence about how we resolve civil disputes from which to judge us, what an odd and troubling view she would have.

Cases filed shows us a bigoted, sexist, racist, mean-spirited, careless, fraudulent, heartless, pornographic, thieving, people who do not honor our obligations. Or at least, as alleged.

Of course, this slice of life does not include other dispute resolution fora such as those that handle domestic, criminal, administrative, workers' compensation and other civil disputes. Though viewing those as well would not likely give our alien visitor a more favorable impression of us.

This accounts for only a fraction of the billions of our annual personal and commercial interactions, most of which proceed peacefully, without dispute. Perhaps this mirror is more like that in a fun house, distorting reality. One can only hope.

Civil disputes in a complex society are inevitable and we are part of a system which purports and strives to resolve them fairly, expeditiously and economically so as to maintain peace, order, freedom, expansion of commerce and the pursuit of happiness. But our system is in danger of failing to achieve those noble goals by systematically excluding many who require it.

Fortunately, we resolve most disputes without lawyers or litigation, and even when we must engage, we seldom require final adjudication by judge or jury. If the civil disputes that went to trial increased by even one percentage point, the system would grind to a halt.

---

[19] The Philadelphia Lawyer, Vol. 78, No.1, Spring 2015

At some point, we all should be required to hire a lawyer and, more importantly, to pay a lawyer's bill. While sending legal bills and even handling client complaints about same can be enlightening, there is nothing quite like having to receive and pay another lawyer's bill. You will quickly come to believe that the cost of civil justice is too high.

Perhaps we have raised Due Process as societal value above all others instead of balancing it against limited time, money, and resources. Federal Judge Ernest Tidwell (N.D. Ga.), once told me of defendant counterfeiters, when I expressed concern in an ex parte application, as he signed my proposed Injunction, "Counsellor, this is all the process they're due."

As a litigator of Intellectual Property disputes I earn my living based on civil disputes and as such am most familiar with the extraordinary costs of these battles. Though over 5,000 Patent Infringement complaints are filed each year, only about 200 actually go to jury verdict. There is good reason for this.

The American Intellectual Property Law Association most recent Report of Economic Survey says that the median cost to litigate a patent dispute with $1-$10 Million at risk is $2 Million and $5 Million when more than $25 Million is at risk. Other similar surveys, such as those done by the National Center for State Courts (ncsc.org) and the American Board of Trial Advocates (abota.org) show similar commercial litigation is seldom less expensive.

Does it really have to cost so much to render justice in such disputes? Or in any disputes?

The Constitution authorizes The Congress "To promote the Progress of Science and useful Arts, by securing for limited Times to Authors and Inventors the Exclusive Right to their respective Writings and Discoveries," but a dispute resolution system which is so costly may not be promoting such "Progress," it may, in fact, be inhibiting it.

And, while the Fifth Amendment provides that no person "be deprived of … property, without due process of law," a prohibitively expensive civil justice system hardly does so.

The Pennsylvania Rules of Professional Conduct impose duties on us not to abuse legal proceedings (R.3.1), not to wrongfully obstruct (R.3.4(a)) and to expedite litigation (R.32), yet none specifically require us to create and implement innovations to minimize the cost of litigation. Our Rules of Civil Procedure impose a duty that we not present anything "for any improper purpose such as to …needlessly increase the cost of litigation," F.R.Civ.P.11(a)(1) and PA.R.Civ.P. 1023(1)(c)(1), but you will search in vain for cases in which courts have sanctioned for violating same, at least not for that reason alone.

I do not pretend to address the equally serious problem of the almost 400,000 in this city living in poverty unable to access the system in any meaningful way. This Bar Association's Civil Gideon and Access to Justice Task Force and others continue this noble fight.

My focus here is on individuals and small and non-Fortune 500 businesses, those who comprise the bulk of the producers in this nation.

In no particular order, I posit seven possible remedies: 1) Alternative Fee Arrangements, 2) Loser Pays, 3) Early Mediation, 4) Accountable Arbitration, 5) "Grand Bargain" Model, 6) "Feinberg" Model, and 7) Closer Court Control.

Some say the days of the Hourly Rate are numbered. Whether true or not, we have entered a new era in which clients of all types are demand creative solutions to mushrooming legal fees. The variety of Alternative Fee Arrangements is only limited by our creativity and willingness to take risk. If nothing else, competition requires that we look here.

The British Rule of Loser Pays has a long and venerable history, though only two states, Alaska and Texas, have adopted any version, both watered-down. While not appropriate for all types of disputes, for some it seems ideal.

Federal Courts in California and Florida have Mandatory Early Mediation with mediators experienced in the area of law at hand. I was, at first, quite skeptical but have resolved many cases in both venues, early and economically, and am now a true believer.

Arbitration, once thought the panacea for all our litigation woes, often now involves greater expense and lacks any accountability, souring many. A recommitment to speed and economy seems necessary along with provision for accountability, such as appellate review for errors of law.

This year, the 100th Anniversary of the Pennsylvania Worker's Compensation Law, we celebrate the prime example of a societal "Grand Bargain" in which workers give up chance of recovery of unlimited compensation in litigation, for the certainty of recovery of fixed compensation. This originally innovative model has worked and has real possibilities for application in other areas.

Kenneth Feinberg, a legendary figure in Alternative Dispute Resolution, has (almost) perfected a model for resolving mass disputes used with the September 11th Fund, the BP Deepwater Horizon Fund and others. While also not applicable to all types of disputes, "The Feinberg Model" has proven an effective, economical method of handling many. It, too, must be considered for broader application.

And last, but not at all least, there is a dire need for closer control by courts, in particular, of discovery. Whether it be by Rule 11 or similar tools or by better scheduling control, something must be done. There was a time when I did not wish two things on my worst enemies – back problems and divorce. I have now added Electronic Discovery to that list.

This new tool of torture has become the discovery tail which wags the merits dog. Whether a document has been preserved and produced has become more important than its possible content, "Spoliation!" has become the Rebel Yell of the Litigation Tactic Du Jour. At astounding expense, we gather and produce millions of documents, only to have a handful actually used. Delaware Federal Judge Sue L. Robinson observed, that in 9 patent trials over which she presided, only an average of <u>87</u> documents were admitted.

The 'elephant in the room' (or sacred cow) here is legal fees. The expense of discovery services, investigators and experts can be exorbitant, but the overwhelming factor is our fees. The practice of law is a profession, and a noble and honorable one at that, but, we must acknowledge that it is <u>also</u>, and has always been, for most, a business.

We must strike the proper balance between making our courts economically accessible to all who require dispute resolution <u>and</u> providing sufficient compensation to advocates to ensure quality and honorable representation. This requires innovative thinking, experimentation and bold leadership. Unless we act with purpose and dispatch, there is a very real risk that just resolution of important civil disputes will be available only to the wealthy, the insured and those with contingent or statutory fee recovery.

Until we can, as Rodney King pleaded, "all just get along," we will require civil courts to adjudicate disputes and we must make them economically accessible to all. Otherwise, the more powerful and well-heeled will win most disputes, even when in the wrong.

"A JUDGE'S PATIENCE – JUDGE FRANKLIN VAN ANTWERPEN"[20]

I was saddened to read of the passing of Judge Franklin S. Van Antwerpen (E.D. PA. U.S.D.Ct.) last week. A true gentleman, professional and outstanding jurist.

I was reminded of the time in 1988 when I had a jury trial before him – his first as a newly minted Federal Judge.

For some reason, Judge Van Antwerpen had been assigned to an old, long disused, musty 2nd floor courtroom in the U.S. Post Building in Easton. It had last been used for the filming of "The Dain Curse," a CBS TV miniseries starring James Coburn in 1978. Although he was happy to tell us all about that brush with Hollywood, the glamour must have worn off as he readily vacated that location for a more modern venue in the new Larry Holmes Building around the block only two years later.

I was defending a nearby borough police department and an officer in a very contentious, emotionally-charged, highly-publicized civil rights case. At the parties' request, Judge Van Antwerpen had ordered all witnesses sequestered so as not to taint any anticipated testimony. Unlike on television, our courtroom was, as most are, virtually empty and I knew those few in the audience were unrelated to the case, only curious observers.

My worthy opponent was a clever fellow whom I suspected might have a surprise or two in store for me. So I was particularly wary.

Towards the end of plaintiff's case, after a lunch break on the second day of trial, I returned to the courtroom a bit early only to find an elderly couple sitting in the rear of the courtroom. Neither I nor my associate recognized them and we had no clue who they were.

---

[20] The Philadelphia Bar Reporter, Vol. 46, No. 2, February 2017

Concerned that they were surprise witnesses or plants for plaintiff, I prepared to raise the issue with the Judge before he had the jury brought in. Suspecting and thus subtly insinuating that something nefarious was afoot, I rather stridently, but respectfully, demanded that these two unidentified persons be removed from the courtroom.

In retrospect, I should have known I was on the wrong track as my opponent expressed total surprise and ignorance. Judge Van Antwerpen simply, politely, said, "Don't worry about them, counselor." Being then still a relatively young lawyer, I did not get the message and persisted with my demand.

Judge Van Antwerpen, again, calmly, but more firmly, told me, "We are going to proceed. No need to be concerned." Still not getting it and now even more suspicious, I, unwisely, pressed the issue again.

A bit amused, ever gracious, but somewhat exasperated with my youthful zeal, Judge Van Antwerpen finally, looked over at his clerk, shook his head and quietly said, "Counselor, they are my parents." "And they have come to watch me preside over my first trial as a Federal Judge."

I turned red, but did not lose my composure, immediately welcoming them and offering to get them coffee. The Judge and his parents laughed and the case proceeded with two new audience members. – Dr. Franklin J. and Dorothy Van Antwerpen.

VI. CHANGES

"1954 - THAT WAS THE YEAR THAT WAS"[21]

My father, born in 1925, turned 86 this year. For his birthday, I gave him a book containing the front page of *The New York Times* for every one of his birthdays. He was amused and delighted to see what happened on the day of his birth each day of his life.

Surely I am not the only one to note this, but when I read history, and I read a lot, I am always amused at important events which occurred in the year of my birth, 1954, or at least the first year of my life, 1954-1955. I just finished two excellent books which cover U.S. history for most of my life – H.W. Brands' American Dreams – The United States Since 1945 and James T. Patterson's Grand Expectations – The United States, 1945-1974. It is strange and eye-opening to realize that prominent historians are writing of the time in which you actually lived as history.

Warren Buffett says 1954 was the best year ever for the stock market. The Dow Jones Average closed at an all-time high of 382.74! High praise from the Oracle of Omaha. Maybe it is because color TV (the RCA-CT-100: sold for $1000) and TV dinners were first introduced. One could dine in front of color TV and watch the new "Tonight Show" with Steve Allen or the first broadcast of the Miss America Pageant. Or maybe it was Elvis Presley's first commercial recording, "That's All Right." Or maybe the introduction of the first antipsychotic drug.

It was a nuclear year. Dwight Eisenhower, hero of WWII, just ended the Korean War the year before, without using nuclear weapons, but we flexed our muscle by exploding the first Hydrogen Bomb on Bikini Atoll in the Marshall Islands. The first atomic power station opened, but as with Sputnik a few years later, it was the Russians who bested us and did it first. Ike later in the year personally switched on the first U.S. nuclear plant while the First

---

[21] The Philadelphia Lawyer, Vol. 77, No. 2, Summer 2014

Lady, Mamie, christened the first nuclear-powered submarine, the USS Nautilus. The Red Scare lead to J. Robert Oppenheimer, "Father of The Atomic Bomb", being stripped of his security clearance.

Secretary of State John Foster Dulles announced our new military policy of "massive retaliation" just about the time Ike wisely decided not to intervene, with nuclear or conventional weapons, to help the doomed 12,000 man French Garrison at Dien Bien Phu in Vietnam. We created the Southeast Asia Treaty Organization (SEATO), a poor imitation of NATO, and supported autocrat Ngo Dinh Diem as Premier of South Vietnam, at least until we sanctioned his assassination a few years later.

General Curtis Le May had over 1,750 war planes in the Strategic Air Command which could deliver nuclear weapons, but Ike preferred to change other regimes in more subtle ways. The CIA covertly intervened in Guatemala to overthrow Col. Jacobs Arbenz Guzman, primarily because he had the audacity to expropriate (though with compensation) lands of the giant U.S. company, United Fruit.

The political left and right were polarizing, but enhancing their intellectual credentials. Irving Howe founded the leftist magazine *Dissent* and William F. Buckley, Jr. founded the right wing journal, *National Review*. For the less cerebral, the first issue of *Sports Illustrated* also came out, though without swimsuits, yet. For the more prurient, *Playboy* appeared featuring the assets of Marilyn Monroe.

Anti-communism and religion were on the rise and many found it necessary to waive the flag and inject God into government. On Flag Day, Ike signed a law adding "one nation under God" to the Pledge of Allegiance and, not to be undone, Congress added "In God We Trust" to our currency. God and country were now officially linked and few mentioned the First Amendment's religious prohibitions.

Khrushchev and Eisenhower met at a "summit" in Geneva, the first such meeting since Truman, Stalin and Churchill met at Potsdam in 1945, but little progress was made. Ike wisely refused to get too involved when the "Red" Chinese shelled the Nationalist Chinese islands of Quemoy and Matsu. While first to express the "Domino Theory", he vowed not to get us in to yet another land war in Asia, though he did double U.S. monetary aid to the French fighting to retain their colonial empire in Southeast Asia.

We seemed to have tired of immigration as we looked inward to reap the material benefits of the post-war boom. Ellis Island welcomed its last "tired, poor, huddled masses yearning to be free" and closed its doors, and the poorly-named government program, "Operation Wetback," sent almost 4 million illegal immigrants back to Mexico.

Post-war youth was already beginning to show a rebellious nature. Marlon Brando in "On The Waterfront" and James Dean in "Rebel Without a Cause" were silver screen harbingers of trouble to come.

Lords reigned in popular literature with the publication of William Golding's Lord of the Flies and J.R.R. Tolkein's first two Lord of the Rings works.

Television and insipid sitcoms inundated virtually every household, but brought serious concerns expressed so well in the best seller, Why Johnny Can't Read. Ray Kroc cut a deal with Dick and Mac McDonald to franchise their fast food restaurants, while competitor Burger King opened its first location. Watching TV while eating high calorie, greasy, fast food seemed like an advance in civilization at the time.

Walt Disney opened his Magical Kingdom of Disneyland in Anaheim, California and we never looked at an amusement park the same way again. Not to be outdone in popular culture by an American mouse, Japan released its first Godzilla movie.

Martin Luther King, Jr., 26, took over as Pastor of the Dexter Avenue Baptist Church in Birmingham just as Chief Justice Earl Warren and a unanimous Supreme Court, in *Brown v. Board of Education* overruled the "separate but equal" doctrine of *Plessy v. Ferguson* holding that separate public schools for whites and blacks are "inherently unequal" and thus unconstitutional. Part-time NAACP employee, Rosa Parks, famously refused to move to 'the back of the bus', leading to the Montgomery Bus Boycott, though the less heralded Claudette Colvin did it nine months earlier.

Red-baiting, Communist hunter, Sen. Joseph McCarthy's witch hunt crashed and burned when he was chastised in the Senate Army-McCarthy Hearings by Boston lawyer Joseph Welch ("Have you no shame, sir?") and excoriated by Edward R. Morrow on TV's "See It Now." For all his bluster, McCarthy never found even one communist in government service.

The Soviets formed the Warsaw Pact locking what Churchill had dubbed The Iron Curtain. Rather than direct confrontation of the "Communist Menace", Eisenhower preferred to follow the recommendations of his top secret, newly-issued Doolittle Commission Report which essentially said that the U.S. had to use covert and illegal means to fight the Communists, or be overwhelmed.

Health, welfare and education were improving markedly. The "Greatest Generation" of veterans was being educated courtesy of the GI Bill. Eisenhower, though Republican, broadened Social Security coverage and extended the minimum wage. And Jonas Salk's nationwide anti-Polio inoculation campaign, begun in Pittsburgh, was a huge success.

Technology advanced at a heady pace. Texas Instruments developed the first transistor radio just in time for teenagers to listen to the new hit by Bill Haley and The Comets, "Rock Around the Clock" featured in the controversial movie, "The Blackboard Jungle." Boeing introduced the first successful commercial jetliner, the 707. On the military front, Lockheed put out the huge YC-130 Hercules transport plane and the F-104

Starfighter, which could do Mach Two. The Soviets countered with the MIG-19, their first supersonic fighter. The jet age was on!

Nature had her say that year. Three major hurricanes, including the worst in the century, Hazel, hit the U.S. But we unlocked some of her secrets when Watson and Crick discovered the DNA double helix and doctors performed the first human organ (kidney) transplant in Boston.

It was a different time economically. Gas was $.22 cents a gallon, a movie ticket was $.70 cents, inflation was only 0.32%, average new car cost $1,700 and the average home cost $10,250.

In sports, Roger Bannister ran the first four minute mile, the Phillies bought Connie Mack Stadium and the Cleveland Browns beat Detroit 56-10 to win the NFL Championship.

Life was more fun as Peanut M&M's, Play Doh and the Fender Stratocaster all made their first appearance in the marketplace.

All was not peace, prosperity and innocence at home, however. Terrorism struck the heart of government when four Puerto Rican Nationalists fired gunshots from the House of Representatives gallery, wounding five Congressmen.

Many who would gain fame in later years were also born in 1954 – Oprah Winfrey, Howard Stern, Christi Brinkley, John Travolta, Ron Howard, Jerry Seinfeld, Sonia Sotomayor, Elvis Costello, Al Sharpton, Condoleezza Rice and Denzel Washington.

All things considered, it was not a bad time and place to be born into. We have come a long way since 1954, but there is so much more to be done. I hope I live to see it.

"REEFER MADNESS REDUX"[22]

Reported sales of legalized "medical" marijuana in the U.S. last year reached $1.8

Billion, just short of sales of America's No. 1 pleasure drug, VIAGRA®. In twenty-three states and the District of Columbia "dealers" have become "caregivers" and "heads" have become "patients." Cheech and Chong are "approved providers." More than a dozen other states are considering such programs, which are favored, according to a recent Gallup Poll, by 70 percent of Americans.

Twenty states and the District of Columbia have actually decriminalized marijuana possession and many localities have effectively done so via ordinance or police and prosecutor discretion. Although in 2013, more than 750,000 people were arrested for possession of small amounts of marijuana at an enforcement cost of $8.7 billion, the latest Pew Research Center Poll say 54 percent of Americans favor legalization. Yet, California in 2010 and Oregon in 2013 defeated such proposals. One report opines that taxing legal sales could produce almost $9 billion in revenue per year. If true, legalization would be a net gain of $18 billion, enough to build more than 1,000 new schools.

Colorado, Washington, Alaska, Oregon and the District of Columbia have legalized marijuana. Although Colorado has a hefty tax, this new natural wonder has already made that state a new tourist destination – the Amsterdam of the Wild West.

In the first five months of this year, Colorado's experiment with 'regulating marijuana like alcohol' (Constitutional Amendment 64) has brought $60 million in new tax revenue and a 77% drop in marijuana prosecutions. Crime and fatal car crashes are down. Life goes on in the Centennial State.

---

[22] The Philadelphia Lawyer, Vol. 78, No. 3, Fall 2015

Despite Philadelphia District Attorney Seth Williams' 2010 decision to stop prosecuting most minor pot possession cases, Philadelphia Police still arrested and detained people in possession of any amount. It is, of course, a classic police tool of control and for discrimination. Pittsburgh and Chicago have long been much more progressive in this regard, issuing only citations with no arrests.

However, in an attempt to stop the senseless arrests of thousands of people a year, Philadelphia City Council passed an ordinance decriminalizing the possession of less than one ounce, and Mayor Nutter approved it last October. Bills permitting sale for "medicinal purposes" are working their way through the Pennsylvania Legislature and Governor Wolf promises to approve. Commentators muse that our State Store system is the perfect vehicle for dispensing pot.

This is a smoking hot issue.

Studies show more than 20 of the 314 million people in the United States use marijuana at least occasionally and over 150 million have inhaled at least once. With that kind of demand, capital, innovation and advocates for legalization are sure to be found. In Canada and the U.K., GW Pharmaceuticals sells SATIVEX®, a cannabis-based nose and mouth spray that might just make "rolling your own" a quaint, archaic phrase.

All of these developments brought to mind my time working for the presidential commission which first recommended nationwide decriminalization of Cannabis Sativa 43 years ago. And, no, I was not a tester.

Those who know me as a life-long liberal Democrat and card-carrying ACLU member are surprised that I once worked for Republican President Richard Milhous Nixon, the man who is said to have referred to my alma mater, Swarthmore College, as "The Kremlin on The Crum." Yes, 'tis true, this bleeding heart, in 1972, was employed as a "Youth Consultant" by President Nixon's National Commission on Marihuana and Drug Abuse. The story begins in a New Orleans hotel room with Maureen E. Biner, later known as Mrs. John Dean.

While attending Jesuit High School in New Orleans in early 1970s, I saw many teenagers, including some close friends, suffer the ravages of drug abuse. I discovered an innovative anti-drug program, The Open Door - C.O.D.E. (Committee on Drug Education) run by an amazing, liberal couple of social workers from Massachusetts, Nick and Judy Katsirubas. Rather than scaring or threatening youngsters with doctor or police speeches or addict testimonials, this program used teenagers, like myself, to inspire younger students to appreciate life sans recreational drugs. I learned much about the drug culture and problem in the city and how to show others the way through or around it.

One day, Nick called to ask me to meet some people who were in town looking into the drug problem. I was to meet these folks at Le Pavillion, then the newest, most elegant hotel in New Orleans, along with two colleagues from the program. Nick had no further information on who these people were. I was just to do my best to help them understand and appreciate the drug problem in the city.

When I arrived at the hotel, I called the room number I had been given. A man answered "Governor Shaefer." Not knowing that he was the former, one-term Republican Governor of Pennsylvania, Raymond P. Shafer (1967-1971), I almost asked, "Governor of what?" but refrained and accepted his invitation to come up to his suite.

In a smartly appointed, spacious suite I found four well-dressed men sitting around a coffee table and a long-legged blonde on the bed. The blonde was Maureen E. Biener, then girlfriend, later wife of White House Counsel John Dean. She was then Executive Assistant to the Executive Director for the entity that these gentlemen served – The President's National Commission on Marihuana and Drug Abuse. Governor Shaefer, its Chairman, was accompanied by Commission members J. Thomas Ungerleider, M.D., Professor of Psychiatry at UCLA; and Mitchell Ware, Esq.,

Superintendent of the Illinois Bureau of Investigation; as well as Michael R. Sonnenreich, Esq., Executive Director of the Commission. An august group to be sure. Turns out they were in town to hold formal hearings on the drug problem in America as they would do in several other cities.

The Commission was established by Nixon in 1971 and tasked with studying the drug problem in America and making recommendations to solve it – the War on Drugs! It had recently issued its first report solely on marijuana that, to Tricky Dick's dismay, recommended decriminalization: Marihuana: A Signal of Misunderstanding (1972, G.P.O.) No surprise to those who knew him well, Nixon never really wanted an independent study of these issues. He reportedly refused to read the first report and told Governor Shaefer, "You're enough of a pro to know that for you to come out with something that would run counter to what the Congress feels and what the country feels, and what we're planning to do would make your Commission look bad as hell." Undaunted, it was then working on its second and final report, one to which I would end up contributing: Drug Use in America: Problem in Perspective (1973, G.P.O.).

My C.O.D.E. compatriots and I spent a couple hours with this group enlightening them on drug abuse in our area from our perspective and what they might expect to hear the next day at the hearings.

As the evening wound down, Executive Director Sonnenreich pulled me aside and asked if I would formally testify at the hearings. I was honored, and, of course, agreed immediately, even though I had no clue what it meant to 'formally testify' before a presidential commission. And I had now agreed to do so in less than 24 hours.

With a little coaching from my lawyer father who had testified before in congressional hearings, I seemed to perform well. After my testimony before the Commission and a packed auditorium at the new J.F.K. High School (every city had one back then), during a break, Sonnenreich again pulled me aside and said, "The

Commission members were impressed with what you said and how you said it. And they would like to appoint you as a Youth Consultant to the Commission to work in Washington, D.C. in the summer." Though stunned, I remained impassive, and simply said, "I would be honored to so serve. Thank you and thank you to the Commissioners."

Securing parental approval, after the fact, I left for Washington D.C. on June 10,1972 to serve my country and my President in my first government job.

I was one of a handful of "Youth Consultants," ostensibly hired to give the middle-aged men and women on this stuffy Commission the "youth" viewpoint of the nation's drug problem and possible solutions. The reality is that we were probably mostly window dressing – so the Commission could say that it had consulted knowledgeable representatives of America's youth. However, the taxpayers got their money's worth because we all worked hard and produced valuable research contributing to the final Commission Report.

I authored a report on "Minimal Brain Dysfunction and Drug Therapy" concluding that, contrary to popular belief, the treatment of MBD (then also called Hyperkenesis, now Attention Deficit Hyperactivity Disorder) in children with stimulants like RITALIN®, did not lead to drug abuse. In fact, to the contrary, it engendered a healthy respect for prescription drugs, if not also aversion to illegal drugs. I also co-authored a report on over-the-counter drugs – "Consumption Patterns of Psychotherapeutic Drugs" and consulted on projects studying high school drug policies, drug adulterants, drug deaths and minority group drug education programs. Not too shabby for a barefoot boy from the bayou.

I lived in a George Washington University dormitory at the corner of 19th Street and Pennsylvania Avenue, two blocks from The White House, one block from the aptly-named C.R.E.E.P. Headquarters (Committee To Re-Elect the President), and a few blocks from the then unknown, but soon to be legendary Watergate. Just seven days after I arrived in D.C. to work for this President, other of his "employees," on the evening of June 17, 1972, were caught burglarizing and bugging the Headquarters of the Democratic National Committee in the Watergate office building. I, along with most of the country, did not appreciate the significance of all the police lights, sirens and activity taking place near my new home that evening. As an innocent 17-year- old, for all I knew this was a normal hot summer night in our nation's capital. Woodward and Bernstein were soon on the case, and, as they say, the rest is history, eventually leading to the resignation of the President for whom I had just started working.

Maureen "Mo" Dean left the Commission in early 1972 and married John Dean that October. She gained fame the next summer as she appeared on TV at the Senate Watergate Hearings, the icy blonde, calmly, coolly standing by her man, as her husband proceeded to spill the beans about Nixon's involvement in and knowledge of the Watergate burglary/bugging and cover up disclosing "the cancer on the Presidency." Dean has written that it was Mo who prompted him to tell the truth about Nixon. She had secured her position with the NCMDA, as many do in Washington, not due solely to her qualifications and credentials, but because she knew someone, or at least was the girlfriend of someone who knew someone. John Dean was friends with Mike Sonnenreich, the NCMDA Executive Director, and had had Sonnenreich appointed to that position. So when John Dean, Counsel to the President, asked him to find a job for Mo, it was a done deal. I had to perform in public for the Commission to get my job.

In 1972, Washington was a small, intimate town with little security. One could walk into almost any building, including the U.S. Capitol, with no security screening. And one often encountered the famous and powerful. One night on my walk home from work, as I stood on a corner of Pennsylvania Avenue, a long, blue limo pulled up to the light right in front of me. Not two feet from me, with window down, sat U.S. Attorney General John Mitchell and his not yet infamous wife, Martha. I said "Good evening, Mrs. Mitchell and Mr. Attorney General," to which they graciously responded, "Good evening, young man." Three years later he would be convicted of obstruction of justice, conspiracy and perjury for his role in the Watergate break-in and cover up. Martha would earn the moniker "Mouth of the South" for her odd statements to the press about Watergate, though much of what she said turned out to be true.

The Commission issued its final report to the President the next year in March 1973, including some of my work. By that time, Nixon was distracted daily with new revelations about Watergate and the final withdrawal of the last U.S. ground troops from Vietnam. As he did with the first Commission Report, Nixon shelved his copy. To my knowledge, few if any of its recommendations were ever implemented. It is, however, nice to see at least one, the decriminalization of marijuana, being resurrected 43 years later.

As Justice Frankfurter observed, "Wisdom too often never comes, and one ought not to reject it merely because it comes late." Henslee v. Union Planters National Bank Trust Co., 335 US 595, 600 (Dissent, 1949).

"CONVENTIONAL WISDOM – THEN AND NOW"[23]

This summer, here, where this nation was created by 56 men 227 years ago, we may witness the first nomination by a major political party of a woman for President. And one who has an excellent chance of becoming the first female President of the United States. Fifteen to twenty thousand journalists are expected to cover the event.

Yes, a few women have run for the office before – Victoria Woodhull (1872 – Equal Rights Party), Linda Jenness (1972 – Socialist Workers' Party) and Jill Stein (2012-Green Party), all nominees of small parties and none on the ballot in all states. And, of course, many others sought their parties' nomination, some first and some famously – Senator Margaret Chase Smith (ME) (1964-Republican Party) and Rep. Shirley Chisolm (NY) (1972-Democratic Party) and some, jokingly – Gracie Allen (CA) (1940-Surprise Party).

This impending potentially historical event so close in time and place reminded me of my experience 40 years ago as a Radio Correspondent at the 1976 Democratic National Convention at Madison Square Garden in New York City.

My love of rock'n'roll, passion for politics and mellifluous "radio voice" had lead me to serve as a disc jockey, news reporter, News Director and eventually Station Manager of WSRN-FM, Swarthmore College's radio station (1972-1976). While my weekly show, "Sensuous Sounds" was a local hit, neither Wolfman Jack nor Casey Kasem were ever threatened.

Our news reporting, based primarily on an "alternative" view of daily events pirated from KYW Radio and the New York Times, was, however, insightful and often amusing.

---

[23] The Philadelphia Lawyer, Vol. 79, No. 1, Spring 2016

Knowing that broadcast journalism was a tough business to enter, I opted for the law instead. But before beginning studying torts and contracts at Penn in September of 1976, I got the opportunity to work as a reporter at the Democratic National Convention for the Suburban Radio News Service (SRNS) Election Unit under the catchy moniker "Elections Radio 76" feeding audio reports to a litany of radio stations around the country, including WCCR-Teleprompter Live and the Associated Press Radio. Armed with highly coveted official DNC Press Credentials and a Convention Floor Pass, a couple of my WSRN cohorts and I took off for the Big Apple.

Like most modern political conventions, this was not a gathering of party leaders to discuss issues, evaluate and ultimately select the best candidate. It was merely an expensive public relations event - with free TV air time. Despite the last minute "Anybody But Carter" movement that perfunctorily put three others into nomination, Jimmy Carter had the nomination sewn up a month before the Ohio Primary.

This was the last time a Vice Presidential nominee (Walter Mondale) was named first at the convention. With few controversies or surprises, two of the three networks abandoned 'gavel to gavel' coverage and presented only key speakers and features. Not until C-Span arrived three years later could political junkies again be sure to feast on entire conventions.

1976 was a watershed political year - the first presidential election year after the first presidential resignation. My former employer, Richard M. Nixon, had resigned on August 9, 1974, due to allegations of "high crimes and misdemeanors" in connection with Watergate. Since Gerald Ford claimed that "our long national nightmare was over" and pardoned "Tricky Dick," the Presidency was then the Democrats' to lose. And at least thirty-one eager Dems threw their hats in the ring, from Jerry Brown to George Wallace. The sublime to the ridiculous.

Feminism was at the forefront of domestic issues and women led this convention. Convention Chairperson

Congresswomen Lindy Boggs (D.-LA) was the first woman ever to preside over a national political convention. Coincidentally, she was my Congressperson. Although I tried several times to interview her, Tom Brokaw and Barbara Walters inexplicably seemed to have more access.

Representative Barbara Jordan (D.-TX) was the first female (and black) Keynote Speaker at any U.S. presidential nominating convention, but even the progressive Democrats made her share the limelight with astronaut hero, white male, Senator John Glenn. The First <u>Co</u>-Keynote Speakers ever. Though Jordan was not actually a candidate, she did receive one vote.

We were poor college students and could hardly afford the pricey hotels of Manhattan, not like the humble peanut farmer, Jimmy Carter in his 21st Floor, $750-a-day, five-room suite at The Americana. After trying, without success, to find a place to crash, we improvised and found a quiet, remote meeting room hallway floor at the Statler Hilton across from The Garden to sleep on between trips back to the Convention Floor. Could have been worse.

Stints in college radio launched the careers of many of the rich and famous, from David Letterman (Ball State-WCRD) to Howard Stern (Boston University-WTBU). At least one of my SRNS convention colleagues, James Rupert, went on to a distinguished career in journalism and now serves as Foreign Affairs Correspondent and Editor for the U.S. Institute of Peace. Another, Ken Hirschkop, used his love of language to become an Associate Professor of English and Literature at the University of Waterloo.

In those pre-Jon Stewart days, even Democrats seemed to have no sense of humor. Comedian-pundit Mark Russell singing harmless ditties at the nearby Rainbow Grill was acceptable, but "The <u>Un</u>official Delegates' Guide to New York City" featuring a centerfold of Elizabeth Ray and Congressman Wayne Hayes in a compromising position, was deemed "tasteless" and "counterproductive" by the DNC and banned.

To add insult to injury, the DNC declared that beer was not to be sold in Madison Square Garden. Cynics claimed it was to boost sales of Georgia-based Coca-Cola® products. Others just smiled, knowing that all manner of other intoxicants would continue to flow in the VIP and Hospitality Lounges. Democratic Fat Cats don't drink beer anyway. And Carter's brother's "Billy Beer" would not be marketed until July of 1977.

In his acceptance speech former Georgia Governor James Earl Carter, Jr. said that 1976 would be "the year when we gave government of this county back to the people of this country." Meant to demean the previous Republican administration, ironically, similar sentiments expressed today by others sound like code for race baiting.

The Equal Rights Amendment, first introduced in Congress in 1923, passed both houses of Congress in 1972, but by this Convention, only 34 of the 38 states needed had ratified it and the deadline for passage was less than three years away. The Democratic Women's Caucus ensured that the Chair of DNC Platform Committee, a young Michael S. Dukakis (Swarthmore '55), included support for ratification.

Unfortunately, few ever read any party platform. Curiously, the 1976 DNC Platform includes a plan for "a comprehensive national health insurance system with universal and mandatory coverage." Thirty-four years later, The Patient Protection and Affordable Care Act was signed into law by a Democratic President. Some things just take time.

Security was tight at The Garden though targeted primarily outside at domestic protestors and nothing like what exists today. Even though only eight years after Robert F. Kennedy and Martin Luther King, Jr. were assassinated, there were no metal detectors and portly rent-a-cops formed the front line of defense. Surely security at the Wells Fargo Center this summer will be substantially greater and targeted primarily at possible foreign threats.

Perhaps the delegates and candidates will reflect on why and how presidential foreign policy decisions over the past 67 years have created, sustained and /or exacerbated some of the security threats we face today.

We forget that we lost our innocence to modern international terrorism in the form of airplane highjackings to Cuba (First-May 1, 1962) caused, in large part, by an embargo which took us 55 years to realize did not work and, in fact, was counterproductive.

My intrepid colleagues and I came to New York armed with liberal passion and the latest technology – a new UHER Report 4000 portable reel-to-reel; two track, stereo tape recorder made by UherWerke of Munich, Germany, the classic tool of professional journalists of the time. WSRN-FM was then the largest and best-funded student organization at Swarthmore, so we had great equipment. Some of us, however, were not so facile with the high technology of the day.

Although this was four years post-Watergate and the concomitant flurry of reform laws, the Convention was still filled with hundreds of lobbyists offering free food, drink and who knows what else to the politicians. Since no lobbyist organization could afford to offend the press, press credentials opened doors to lots of free fine food and drink.

I recall especially the unbelievable endless spread and open bar provided in the Railroad Press Hospitality Lounge. Just a few years later, President Carter signed into law the Staggers Rail Act deregulating American railroads replacing the ICC structure in place since 1887. Watergate did not change everything.

The Convention was a virtual Democratic love fest, especially compared to the acrimony at the 1968 and 1972 conventions. But the Women's Caucus pressed a potentially explosive issue – "the female quota" – equal representation with men in delegations at future conventions. One hot "candidate" who supported it was young, outsider California Governor Jerry Brown.

Eager to avoid a public dispute, Carter's 'Georgia Mafia' deftly brokered a compromise – denying quotas but "encouraging and assisting" efforts to achieve equality. Forty years later, the DNC requires state delegations to have an Affirmative Action Plan, but, still, no quotas.

1976 should have shown progress, but there were actually 3.6% fewer women delegates (34.4% to 38%) and fewer black delegates (11% to 15%) than in 1972. Though both were significant improvements over 1968 (13% women; 5.5% blacks).

For the record, our reporting team was 33⅓% women.

Whether it was that this was the first opportunity to elect a Democrat since Lyndon Johnson, the glitter of the Big Apple or just the presence of so many cameras and microphones, Hollywood was well-represented at The Garden. Fresh off his latest huge success co-authoring and playing the randy hairdresser in "Shampoo," Warren Beatty was a constant presence. Long active in liberal politics, he had in 1972 been part of Democratic Candidate George M. Govern's inner circle raising a great deal of money.

At 6'2", wearing a three-piece white suit, black shirt, no tie, sporting a dazzling smile and a shock of jet black hair, he made quite a spectacle wandering the convention corridors. While a 2010 biography estimated that he had slept with 12,775 women, he seemed more concerned with women's political rights that hot New York summer.

Since the nomination was a foregone conclusion before the convention began, the several thousand journalists present had to find some burning issues upon which to report. Even pre-internet the demand by media outlets for content was ravenous, which explains, in part, why a lowly suburban radio stringer was able to score an in-depth interview with Warren Beatty about women's rights.

We quickly learned that almost anyone would talk to us anytime about anything. Press Credentials and a microphone have an amazing effect on people. No one ever questioned whether we were from a group of local radio stations or a giant network and our Floor Pass Credentials were the same as those of the network anchors.

The star of "Bonnie & Clyde" was equally as willing to answer the impertinent questions of this then 21 year old recent college graduate as he was those of rock star reporter Frank Reynolds of ABC-TV. I encountered Mr. Beatty in a hallway just off the convention floor and asked if I could interview him. He readily agreed and I warmed up my UHER and thought of some tough questions about his support for the Women's Caucus proposal. He was charming, knowledgeable and articulate and I left him with what I thought was about 15 minutes of a great scoop for which I was sure to win accolades from my fellow journalists, if not an Edward R. Murrow Award.

Sadly, my brush with greatness was not recorded. Apparently, I had yet to master the German engineering of my high-tech tape recorder and had only recorded my intro and not a word from Mr. Beatty.

My colleagues honored me for the next few days by calling me 'Rose Mary Woods', Nixon's secretary supposedly responsible for the famous 18 ½ minute gap in a crucial Watergate tape. Woods said she made "a terrible mistake" when she "accidently" hit the 'record' button instead of the 'stop' button on her UHER reel-to-reel tape recorder. Seriously.

I eventually overcame my technology handicap and got a nice interview with the Honorable Father Robert Drinan, S.J., (D. MA)., the first Roman Catholic priest to serve in Congress. Drinan was a brilliant Jesuit law professor who rose to prominence as an anti-war and human rights activist. I must admit that I used both my own Jesuit education and Vietnam War protest credentials to get him to open up. Despite his leadership in a church that hardly favored the feminist agenda, he expressed support for the female delegate proposal.

The 2016 Democratic Convention is likely to be as much of a yawn as that of 1976. The presidential and vice-presidential nominees will already have been selected and there will be no hotly contested platform issues. The novelty and historical significance of either a female or a socialist nominee will be the only attraction.

While 1976 may almost have been "The Year of the Woman," perhaps 2016 will at least be the beginning of the end of the War on Women.

VII. THE CLOWN

"TRUMP WORLD – BE AFRAID. BE VERY AFRAID"

11/8/16 – Donald John Trump elected 45th President of the United States.

- 60.2% of Eligible Voters voted. 39.8% did not vote.
- 26.3% of Eligible Voters voted for Trump – [(lower % than voted for Hitler for President of Germany in 1932 (27.2%)].
- 73.7% of Eligible Voters did not vote for Trump.
- Clinton won popular vote by over 2.8 million.
- 18.5% of 325 million U.S. citizens voted for Trump.
- Fate of 265 million other Americans and perhaps other 7 billion people on the planet determined by a small minority of Americans and a tiny minority of the world.

THE INTERREGNUM – BEFORE THE STORM

DAY ONE

- Shock. Disbelief. Disgust.
- Post-election protests in streets – first in U.S. history.
- Prior Trump claims of rigged election mysteriously cease.

DAY TWO

- Trump meets Obama. Obama looks like he ate a bad oyster. Trump like a deer caught in the headlights. Awkward.
- Trump tweets that protesters are paid professionals incited by media and "very unfair." No evidence.
- Trump looks nervous. The world waits.

DAY THREE

- Trump now tweets praise for protesters. Bipolar?
- Cosby-like, Trump tries to delay his upcoming Fraud Trial.
- Trump changes position on Obama Care – now favors two key provisions: Pre-existing Condition and Child Coverage to 26.
- Trump surrogate Newt Gingrich says promise to make Mexico pay for The Wall was "a great campaign device."

DAY FOUR

- Trump surrogate Rudy Giuliani says tax cuts (for wealthy) first priority. Surprise.
- Trump hires lobbyists whose profession he excoriated in campaign. Big surprise.

DAY FIVE

- Trump says The Wall might now be part "fence." Pink Floyd groans.
- Trump says "Don't be afraid." If he has to say it, be afraid. Be very afraid.
- Trump says he prefers election by popular vote. "President-Elect" Hillary Clinton agrees.
- Trump promised to 'Drain the Swamp.' Appoints Creature From The Black Lagoon, Steve Bannon as Chief Strategist.

DAY SEVEN

- Trump tweets claiming he got Ford to keep plant in Kentucky. Ford never planned to move it. Duh.

- Trump appoints National Security Advisor General Michael Flynn who believes Islam is not a religion, merely a "political ideology." Flynn dusts off General Buck Turgidson's Doomsday Plan from Dr. Strangelove.
- Alabama Senator Jeff Beauregard Sessions III rejected for federal judgeship as racist, whistling "Dixie" as Attorney General. Heard to exclaim "Boy!", but turns out he was just ordering another mint julep.

DAY NINE

- Key Trump supporter Carl Higbie calls for Muslim Registry based on WWII Japanese internment camps precedent. Fred Korematsu from the grave, says, " I told you so."
- Trump promises to deport 2-3 of 11 million unauthorized immigrants. Only 300,000 have felony records. Math never his strong suit.

DAY TEN

- Donald "I Never Settle" Trump settles Trump "University" fraud claims for $25 Million avoiding testimony under oath. TRUTH called from an undisclosed location saying, "I am still here. If anyone cares."
- War Criminal Henry Kissinger consults notes on the 1815 Congress of Vienna (some say he was there) to advise Trump how to remake the world into "TrumpWorld."
- Pence booed and lectured at "Hamilton"; Trump demands cast apologize. Kelly Anne Conway has to explain to him what "apologize" means.
- Trump considers top position for eternal, yet flawed, loyalists Giuliani and Christie. Secretary of Transportation for Christie? Secretary of Fake News, Rumors and Innuendo for Rudy?

DAY ELEVEN

- In call to President of Argentina, Trump suggests he look into government permit problems Trump businesses having there. Really. Surprise?
- Trump proposes a TV game show '2 to 1' Rule for Federal Regulations – drop 2 for every 1 new one. "I'll take Door #3, Donald!"
- SNL nails it on Trump Transition, but Trump tweets it's "not funny." Worst Presidential sense of humor since "Silent Cal" Coolidge.

DAY TWELVE

- Pundits discover Constitution's Emoluments Clause (Art. I, Sec. 9, ¶8) to address Trump's shady dealings with foreign governments. If he starts quartering troops in Black, Latino and Muslim homes, we have a Clause for that too.
- Trump summons media moguls to The Tower (of Terror?) and excoriates the bunch who appear cowed. Upon exit, a school girl reminds them which Amendment is The First.
- Trump cancels New York Times interview claiming the 119 time Pulitzer Prize winner is "biased and unfair."
- Trump announces he will not further prosecute Clintons. For anything. Also, not Ted Cruz's father for the Kennedy assassination. Giuliani and Christie quietly tell him such decisions not within presidential power.
- Trump says "A President cannot have conflicts of interest." Or, as Nixon put it, "When the President does it, it's not illegal." Sigh.

DAY THIRTEEN

- Trump recants and sits for New York Times interview:

- says he thinks he can broker Palestinian-Israeli peace; Jared "Settlements 'R' Us" Kushner throws up a little bit in his mouth.
- says there just might be something to this global warming thing that 99.5% of scientists concur on. Duh.
- says waterboarding may not be as effective as beer and cigarettes. Neglects to say it is also illegal and wrong.
- Ben Carson, M.D. said to be likely for Secretary of Housing and Urban Development. Experience – "I grew up in the inner city." Hey, Brownie did "a heck of a job" in Katrina, didn't he?

- Trump appoints Nikki Haley U.N. Ambassador. Only Republican immigrant offspring he knows. And at least she has an "American" name. Not Patel or Gupta.
- Trump nominates Billionaire (#1) Betsy DeVos Secretary of Education. Does not believe in public schools. Really.

DAY FOURTEEN

- Trump nominates Billionaire (#2) William "King of Bankruptcy" Ross Commerce Secretary. Must be good. Trump was only a "Prince."

DAY FIFTEEN

- NYT reports TrumpWorld includes at least 75 pending Trump lawsuits with more to come if he fulfills pledge to sue 11+ women who accused him of sexual assault. Maybe just the "Trump Full Employment for Lawyers Act."
- Trump says same sex marriage is "settled law" (Obergefell v. Hodges, 2015), but abortion rights are not (Roe v. Wade, 1973). Constitutional scholars across the country express dismay. Then cry.

- Robin Leach announces, "In the next four years, it will be OK to be rich again!" Jordan Belfort considered to head the Securities and Exchange Commission.

DAY SIXTEEN

- In call with British Politician Nigel Farage (U.K.'s version of Herr Trump), Trump asks him to oppose wind farms near a Trump golf course in Scotland. Mixing the people's business with his own. Welcome to TrumpWorld!
- Trump meets with Indian developers about expanding his real estate partnerships in India. 182 million Pakistanis get nervous.

DAY SEVENTEEN

- Trump Organization expands into Saudi Arabia. 8 million Israelies get nervous.
- Foreign diplomats flock to new Trump International Hotel in D.C. hoping to curry favor with The Donald. Muslim diplomats must, however, be "extremely vetted," through rear entrance. Also, no room service for them.
- Castro dies. Trump says he hopes for freedom for the Cuban people. 65.8 million U.S. voters hope for same – for the American people.
- Trump calls recount effort in 3 key states "a scam." Like that "rigged" election he "won." "TrumpWorld – a Different Kind of Truth®."
- Trump refuses to take recommended intelligence briefings. There are none so blind as those who will not see.
- Trump tweets that millions voted illegally. No evidence. Other than, perhaps, the fact of his own "election."

DAY NINETEEN

- General Petraeus emerges as likely Trump State Department pick. Trump appreciates a guy who can keep state secrets in pillow talk, not private server e-mails.

DAY TWENTY

- Trump threatens to jail and/or cancel citizenship of anyone who burns American Flag. Even his legal brain trust, Rudy and The Fat Man, know Supreme Court has held such acts protected by First Amendment and citizenship cannot be revoked as penalty.
- Trump did not know the significance of the 13 stripes in the American flag. Or the stars. Or the colors. Don't get me started on the Constitution.

DAY TWENTY-ONE

- Washington Post lists 282 Major Promises Trump made in Campaign. Only 1.2 per week in first term. Piece of cake for Super Trump!

DAY TWENTY-TWO

- Billionaire (#3) Steve Mnuchin, "King of Foreclosures," tapped to head Treasury Department. Alexander Hamilton considers rising from the grave. But cannot get tickets to his eponymous musical.
- Barney Frank (of Dodd-Frank) says Wall Street has not been this happy since Harding made Andrew Mellon Secretary of Treasury in 1921. Wow, that worked out so well! Can you say, "The Great Depression."?
- Trump gets Carrier to keep in Indiana 730 of 1,400 jobs it was planning to move to Mexico. V.P. Elect Gov. (Ind.) Pence gives $7 million + incentives. Parent company United Technologies just smiles knowing Trump's first legislation will be a tax reduction worth ten times any

savings it would have made by the job move. Smoke, meet mirrors.

DAY TWENTY-THREE

- Trump appoints General James "Mad Dog" Mattis Secretary of Defense. "Mad Dog" led the U.S. Middle East military effort in 2010-13. Which Trump often said was a disaster. Take comfort – Trump says he knows more than all the generals. Right.
- Trump expresses admiration for Kazakhstan despot Nazarbayev in call. Who's next? Der Furher and Il Duce just victims of biased press?
- Trump's Cabinet shaping up as Wall Street not Main Street. Billionaires Mnuchin and Ross are, like Trump, twice divorced, with trophy #3's. Trump can relate.
- Trump lawyers move to block recounts stating "there is no evidence." Forgot to consult their client who claims "millions voted illegally." Even Biff Tannen says, "Butthead!"

DAY TWENTY-FOUR

- Trump takes call from Taiwanese President. China goes ballistic. Well, not literally. Yet. Like a child, he just doesn't know any better.

DAY TWENTY-FIVE

- One guy on Trump Transition Team dealing with 17 intelligence agencies. Senior Official says Briefing Books are "waiting for someone to read them." Maybe they're waiting for the movie. "White House Down"?
- Trump meets with Al Gore to get to the bottom of this Chinese conspiracy on climate change. Mar-a-Lago sinks further into ocean.

DAY TWENTY-SIX

- Trump threatens huge tariff on imports from companies which move facilities/jobs overseas. Ryan reminds him there are two other branches of government. Smoot and Hawley smile and puff on cigars.
- No Trumpster, including VP Elect Mike Pence and Mouthpiece Kelly Anne Conway, acknowledge that there is no evidence of Trump's claim that "millions voted illegally." New Rule #1 in TrumpWorld – "When Trump says it, it is so. No evidence required." Where is that little boy who said "The Emperor has no clothes" when you need him?

DAY TWENTY-SEVEN

- Trump National Security Advisor designee and his Chief of Staff (his son) posit New Rule #2 in TrumpWorld – "rumors and conspiracy theories are true until proven otherwise." N.B., Official End of The Age of Reason.
- Carrier Union President says Trump "lied his ass off." Hmmm… white working class leaders realize Trump speaks not the truth. My heart be still…

DAY TWENTY-EIGHT

- Trump appoints oil and gas industry darling and climate change denier, Oklahoma Attorney General Scott Pruitt head of Environmental Protection Agency. "Make America Cough and Wheeze Again." In other news, Fox appointed Hen House Guard.
- There it is. Trump blames Carrier workers for Carrier moving jobs to Mexico. How many times can we say, "Wow!"
- TIME Magazine names Trump "Person of the Year." In "good" company – Hitler (1938), Stalin (1939 and 1942), Khruschev (1958) and Ayatollah Khomeini (1979).

DAY TWENTY-NINE

- Trump selects fast-food chain exec CKE Restaurants Andy Pudzer to run Department of Labor. Pudzer detests minimum wage and any regulations which protect workers. Probably thinking of getting rid of that pesky, job-killing Thirteenth Amendment, too.
- Trump announces he will remain as Executive Producer of "Celebrity Apprentice." Part-time President might not be a bad thing. Bush #2 did least harm during 1,024 vacation days spent clearing brush in Crawford, Texas.

DAY THIRTY

- Trump now says he will not deport the 700,000 "Dreamers" who entered country illegally as children. Contrary to campaign promises. TrumpWorld! Like a box of chocolates. You never know what you're going to get.
- Trump says he does not believe the 16 U.S. intelligence agencies which conclude that Russia hacked the DNC. Putin pats him on the head, gives him a treat and says, "Good boy, Donald!" Bush lap dog Tony Blair says, "I feel his pain."
- Trump appoints World Wrestling Federation executive Linda McMahon head of Small Business Administration. "Let's get ready to rummmmble... ." Ask Minnesota how well it worked out to elect wrestler Jesse Ventura governor. Then consult George Santayana.

DAY THIRTY-ONE

- Trump claims one of the largest Electoral College victories ever. Before Electoral College even votes. Not so. Only 46th largest. Out of 58.

- Putin Pal Exxon CEO Rex Tillerson, nominated for Secretary of State. Dos va donya. Moscow on the Potomac.
- At rally where Trumpster Zombies chant, "Lock her up!", Trump says, "That plays great before the election. Now, we don't care." Clown-in-Chief. Sigh.

DAY THIRTY-TWO

- Trump put $65 million of his own money into his campaign. Not the $100 million he repeatedly said he would. And his campaign paid back $12 million to his own companies. So he really only put up about half of what he promised. Half the Truth. In TrumpWorld, that's better than average.
- Four of Trump's cabinet appointees made six figure contributions to his campaign. So much for draining the swamp. More like stocking it.

DAY THIRTY-THREE

- CIA study reports Russia intervened to elect Trump. Trump says he doesn't believe it. But then, he does know more than the Generals, the CIA and everyone else on the planet. Didn't you know this guy in junior high? From Russia With Love.

DAY THIRTY-FOUR

- Trump appoints Rick Perry Secretary of Energy. In 2011, Perry said if President, he would eliminate three departments – Commerce, Education, and ... he could not remember the third. Yes, you guessed it – Energy. As Perry said, "Oops."

DAY THIRTY-FIVE

- Trump accuses Obama of withholding info on Russian hacking until after election. Of course, he did not. TRUTH calls again, "Can you hear me now?"
- On his "Thank You" (or "Screw You") Tour, Trump says he is not a "normal American." Ya think? Even a broken clock is right twice a day.
- Ivanka to handle duties of First Lady. Makes sense. Trump said he would date her if she were not his daughter. And having a First Lady who speaks Russian might raise eyebrows.

DAY THIRTY-SIX

- Trump's pick for Ambassador to Israel is a militant, Orthodox Jewish bankruptcy lawyer without any diplomatic experience. Oy, vey! Nothing like reaching out and touching the Arab world.
- Trump tweets that China's seizure of U.S. sea drone is "unpresidented." Wish we could be unpresidented-elect. Use of malaprops is the least of our worries. That he believes this unprecedented is what is really frightening. Those who cannot remember the past are doomed to repeat it. And it seems we may be doomed right along with him.
- In an "unpresidented" move, Trump tweets China to keep the US. Navy drone. We may have now entered The Bizarro World ruled by The Bizarro Code, "Us do opposite of all earthly things!"
- Trump continues to refuse to acknowledge Russian hacking. Only one other American also in denial - that 400 lb guy in his bed in New Jersey. Good company. Putin's Poodle and The Fat Guy.
- Trump demands evidence of Russian hacking. And refuses daily intelligence briefings. There is a reason they are called "intelligence" briefings.

DAY THIRTY-SEVEN

- Trump says recent terrorist events require civilized world to do "new thinking." He hasn't done any, new or old, in years so everyone starts fresh.
- Ethically-challenged TrumpWorld denizen Newt Gingrich suggest Trump pardon (prospectively or periodically) his family and staff so they can do with impunity what is illegal for others. Now, class, please turn to Article II, Section 4 of the Constitution ... Impeachment.
- Trump's 17 Cabinet picks alone have more wealth than 1/3 of all American households. Surely they will help the working class! Right.
- Donald, Jr. (Uday) and Eric (Qusay) Trump have formed the Opening Day Foundation to sell access to the President-elect for millions. Just after they pressured Kuwaiti Ambassador to move huge reception to Trump International Hotel. Qusay Hussein were sent to Hell by the 101st Airborne in 2003. Hmm.... an idea ...

DAY THIRTY-EIGHT

- Electoral College makes it official. Trump 306; Clinton 232. Faith Spotted Eagle 1; Bernie Sanders 1; John Kasich 1; Ron Paul 1, Colin Powell 3. If Electoral College actually operated as intended (See, Federalist #68) we might be inaugurating President Colin Powell on January 20th. Or President Faith Spotted Eagle.
- Trump National Security Advisor Flynn meets with ultra right wing Austrian nationalists. All wearing brown shirts. Next stop – an isolated retirement home in Argentina to gab with some old pals.
- Impeachment talk heats up even before Trump impeachable. Parallels with Andrew Johnson are too many and too spot on to be funny. But Johnson, had better suits. He actually made his own. In America. Unlike Trump.

- Trump promised a $1 Trillion infrastructure building plan. Now Chief of Staff and GOP Senate Leader say it is not going to happen. P.T. Barnum said, "There's a sucker born every minute." Well, maybe 62,979,636.
- Billionaire Carl Icahn appointed Trump Advisor. That's #4!
- Parroting Putin, Trump demands more nukes. A new Arms Race. Wow. Back to The Past-1950's. In more ways than one, Merchants of Death around the globe celebrate. Bomb shelter construction boom.

DAY THIRTY-NINE

- Kelly Ann Conway to be Consigliere. Hope she will be more Hagen than Genco. At least, someone can speak both Trumpese and English!

- Trump announces plan to shut down his "charitable" foundation. No needy notice as it never gave any money away. Well, yes, to settle lawsuits against for-profit Trump entities. And to buy a 6' portrait of 'Our Founder! Picky, picky.

DAY FORTY

- Trump Transition Team makes odd requests of EPA and State Dept. about employees involved in a global warming and gender equality issues. Megalomaniacal autocrats making lists of names never bodes well.

DAY FORTY-ONE

- Trump touts goods "Made in America" while his and Ivanka's branded goods are made in Vietnam, Pakistan, Bangladesh, China, Indonesia, South Africa. Though he says the U.N. is just a "club for people to have a good time," maybe he places orders there for all those "Made in America" Trump goods.

- Rudy, Chris and Newt remain out of Trump administration. Time to dust off that script for remake of "The Three Stooges"?
- Kerry says Israeli Settlements obstacle to peace. Trump tells Israel "Stay strong ... January 20th is fast approaching." Plans for Trump Tower Jerusalem proceed apace. Palestinians need not worry – plenty of bellhop and maid jobs!

DAY FORTY-TWO

- Trump appoints his company's General Counsel, Orthodox Jew, Jason Dov Greenblatt point man for international negotiations, primarily on Israeli-Palestinian of issues. Guess we know where this is going.
- Trump parties with Rocky and Fabio at Mar-A-Lago. The Hulk and Dirty Harry were otherwise engaged. Nero called, "At least he was not fiddling."

DAY FORTY-THREE

- Trump disbelieves all 17 U.S. intelligence agencies which say Russia behind hacking saying "I know things that other people do not know." Yep, we all knew this guy in junior high.
- Trump's Republican House first act – attempt to emasculate House Ethics Office. Guess we see where this is going.

DAY FORTY-FOUR

- Trump claims credit for Ford canceling plans for Mexican plant. Ford says it was due to decreased demand for small cars. He may not be a politician but he has learned their First Rule, "Take credit for everything and blame for nothing."
- After claiming "he knows things" 17 U.S. intelligence agencies do not, then promising to disclose this info,

Trump fails to deliver. Ok, now we really, really, really should get it. How do you know Trump is lying? His lips are moving. Bodes well for those 282 campaign promises. (See Day 21 above)

- Trump praises fugitive Julian Assange and thug Putin. With friends like this, who needs enemies? P.S., Is this your President?
- Trump hires Omarosa for White House staff. Snooky and The Situation also being considered. Her first task – locate Trump's "black guy." And then – a unicorn.
- Team Trump urges Republican Congress to use U.S. tax payer money to pay for The Wall. Can I say it now? Wait for it … "I told you so."
- In break with precedent (and president), Trump demands all Ambassadors resign by Inauguration Day. NYT officially retires phrase "in break with precedent" for use in Trump stories. News Rule #1 – Never state the obvious.
- NYT Editorial "Mr. Trump Casts Intelligence Aside." It had to come. He had already done it with Truth, Decorum, Respect and Honor.

DAY FORTY-FIVE

- Trump receives full intel briefing on Putin's hacking. The Siberian Candidate maintains his bromance, evidence be damned.

DAY FORTY-SIX

- Senate Republicans push to confirm Trump nominees without complete background checks and ethics clearances. Rule of Law calls, "Hey, remember me!"

DAY FORTY-SEVEN

- Trump again denies mocking disabled reporter despite the entire rest of the world seeing it with their own eyes.

Then there were the NY Dancing Muslims on 9/11, evidence of President Obama's real birthplace, secret info on hacking, and on and on... "you've just crossed over into The Twilight Zone."

And now he is the President. Fasten your seatbelts, it's going to be a bumpy ride.

"ONCE A WEEK"[24]

If President Donald J. Trump serves a full four-year term (U.S. Constitution, Art. II, Sec. 1) (a big if), he will serve a total of 208 weeks and five days. For each of those ten score and 8 weeks, he will receive, from me, via U.S. Postal Service (Art. I, Sec. 9, Cl. 7), a pocket- sized, numbered copy of the United States Constitution provided free of charge by the Pennsylvania Bar Association and the Pennsylvania Bar Foundation.

I mailed the first on Inauguration Day, January 20, 2017, and I have sent him 6 more to date. I simply include my card and a Bar Foundation bookmark bearing Benjamin Franklin's now eerily timely quote, "A Republic ... if you can keep it."

I have not yet received a response. Nor have I seen or heard any indication that he has read it. Ever. While not holding my breath, I will continue to send one every Friday, for the next 202 weeks. If he remains in office. And if we all survive.

You may say this is futile and that the 208 pocket Constitutions will be dutifully filed away with all the other "negative" mail he receives. Perhaps they will someday merit their own box on a shelf in the "Donald J. Trump Presidential Library." Dusty and still unread, to be discovered by some presidential historian years from now, to be mentioned only in a footnote of some tome about how this nation got collectively drunk one night and woke up the next day with President Trump.

It is well to remember that the Constitution requires that "Before he enter on the Execution of his Office, he shall take the following Oath or Affirmation:

"I do solemnly swear (or affirm) that I will faithfully execute the Office of the President of the United States, and will to

---

[24] The Philadelphia Lawyer, Vol. 80, No. 2, Summer 2017

the best of my Ability, preserve, protect and defend the Constitution of the United States." (Art. II, Sec. 1, Cl.8)

And he did so. At noon on January 20, 2017. A moment that may live in infamy.

One would think that he would have read it by then. Or by now.

After all, it is what he swore to preserve, protect and defend. And it is "the supreme Law of the Land." (Art. VI, Cl.2)

While it is longer than a 140-character tweet (about 25 words), it is only 7,591 words in length, including all 27 amendments. Assuming he is an average reader, at 200 words per minute, it would only take him 38 minutes to read the whole thing. About the time it takes to play 3 holes of golf at a Trump course. Or do his hair.

While scores of his statements, speeches, tweets, and policies evidence that he has no clue what the Constitution says or means, you may say that he is not a lawyer or a Constitutional scholar. But since he took an oath to it and it is the foundation of the Republic he leads, is it not too much to ask that he sit down one night and actually read it?

If he did, he at least would not make such fundamental errors as the following.

In a meeting last July with House Republicans, Trump said he wants to protect Article XII. But there is no Article XII. The Constitution has only 7 articles and 27 amendments. On "Meet the Press," he told Chuck Todd that the Constitution does not provide for birthright citizenship. Clearly he has not read the first sentence of Section 1 of Amendment XIV.

I have always found it curious that the oath is "to preserve, protect and defend" the Constitution, not the people or the nation. And certainly not his presidency, his political party, his power, his businesses, or his family.

James Madison's <u>Notes of Debates in the Federal Convention of 1787</u> reports that the Committee of Detail draft delivered to the Constitutional Convention by John Rutledge (S.C.) on August 6, 1787 included a required presidential oath, but only the first part of what was eventually agreed to. A few weeks later, on August 27, 1787, Madison (Va) and Col. George Mason (Va) moved to add:

"and will to the best of my judgment and power preserve protect and defend the Constitution of the U.S."

While James Wilson (Pa.) thought it unnecessary, the motion passed 7 to 1, with 2 abstentions (Mass and NC.) Delaware voted No.

Madison's <u>Notes</u> cites to a "draft as finally agreed to" on September 17, 1787 which includes the second part of the oath using the word "judgment, and power," but not "ability." But shortly thereafter, "Ability" was substituted so as to diminish the power of a president's "judgment" in deference to the Constitution. It is the only sentence in the Constitution in quotes. Madison, its principal author, Father of the Constitution, took it himself twice – 1809 and 1813.

While that change is significant, there remains a qualifying phase which could prove to be troubling – "to the best of my Ability." Well, if one is unable/unfit, what good does the oath do? The Constitution and the Republic would be in jeopardy.

Fortunately, there are other self-preservation provisions of the Constitution which can save it (and us), should saving be required. Of course there is the nuclear option – impeachment for "Treason, Bribery, or other high Crimes and Misdemeanors" (Article II, Section 4). Two Presidents have been impeached – Andrew Johnson and Bill Clinton, but none convicted. Since conviction requires a 2/3 vote of the Senate after trial (Article

1, Section 3, C1. 6) and President Trump's Republican Party holds a majority of the seats, impeachment and conviction are very unlikely. Unless the President goes completely off the rails and/or Republicans put country (if not planet) before party, tax cuts for the wealthy, and deregulation of business.

Then there is the little-known and never-used (except in movies) Section 4 of the 25th Amendment, ratified in 1967. In the event that the Vice President and a majority of Cabinet members (now 8 of 15) transmit to the President pro tempore of the Senate and the speaker of the House of Representatives "their written declaration that the President is unable to discharge the powers and the duties of his office," "the Vice President shall immediately assume the powers and duties of the office as Acting President."

Acting President Pence. Not sure that sounds any less disconcerting than President Trump.

But to this "coup d'etat" provision is a "counter-coup" clause. At any time thereafter during his term, the President can transmit his own Declaration "that no inability exists" and automatically "resume the powers and duties of his office."

But wait. There is another catch – he can do so, "unless" the Vice President and majority of the Cabinet "within four days" transmit a Second Declaration that he is "unable."

At that point, or "thereupon," as the Amendment says, "Congress shall decide the issue," Unless 2/3 of both Houses determine he is "unable," "the President shall resume the powers and duties of his office."

As with Impeachment, this is very unlikely to happen, considering the apparent loyalty of Vice President Pence and the Cabinet generals and billionaires and that Republicans comfortably control both houses.

But a man's reach should exceed his grasp ... or what's a Republic for?

Last summer, here in the Cradle of Liberty, not 5 miles from where the Founders completed their work on our Constitution, Khizr Khan, a Muslim lawyer and father of a U.S. Army captain killed in Iraq, gave a passionate speech on country, sacrifice, liberty and equal protection of the laws. He memorably said, as he waved about his pocket copy of the Constitution:

> "Donald Trump you're asking Americans to trust you with our future. Let me ask you: Have you ever read the U.S. Constitution? I will gladly lend you my copy. In this document, look for the words "liberty" [Preamble; Article V] and "equal protection of law." [Amd. XIV, Sec. 1]

As the Ninth Circuit Court of Appeals decision in *Washington v. Trump*, No. 17-3505, upholding the injunction against his Muslim ban makes painfully clear, Trump has still not read the Constitution.

So, I will keep sending him a copy. Once a week.

"IN THE TRUMP ZONE - THE YEAR OF LIVING DANGEROUSLY"

Millions of words have been and millions more will be written about Trump's first year in office, but sometimes, numbers alone better tell the story. Thus, herein is the digital tale, meticulously researched and supported by credible, substantial evidence. <u>Not</u> "Fake News." Believe me. When he threatens to sue, I will have my defense already prepared. That is, if truth is still a defense. Or has any meaning any more.

I pen this on January 20, 2018, the first anniversary of his inauguration. Despite or perhaps because his party controls all three branches of government, the Federal Government shut down as the clock struck midnight last night.

Ask not for whom the bell tolls. It tolls for thee.

A few caveats. First, as Joe Friday of "Dragnet" would say, "Just the facts, ma'am." Second, this litany is limited to the first 365 days of his presidency. Thus, by the time you read this, these numbers will have changed. And, hopefully, not too awfully. Perhaps, they will even be finalized, as he may no longer be president. One can only hope.

<u>PROMISES, PROMISES</u>

282	•	Campaign Promises Made
7	•	Campaign Promises Kept (2.5%)
60	•	"100 Day" "Contract With The American Voter" Promises Made
7	•	"100 Day" "Contract With The American Voter" Promises Kept (11.6%)
15	•	"100 Day" "Contract With The American Voter" Promises Broken (25%)

LIES

1,950+   •   Material Public Lies and Misrepresentations

CRIME AND PUNISHMENT

4   •   Administration Officials Indicted on Federal Felony Charges

2   •   Administration Officials Plead Guilty to Federal Felony Charges

CRYING WOLF

28   •   Threats To Sue Others

28   •   Threats To Sue Others Not Carried Out

1   •   Threats To Nuke Others

1   •   Threats To Nuke Others Not Carried Out

HIGH CRIMES AND MISDEMEANORS

TBD   •   Attempts To Obstruct Justice

TBD   •   Violation Of U.S. Constitution's Emoluments Clause (Art. II, Sect. 1)

5   •   Personal Defense Lawyers Retained

HELPING HANDS

0   •   Candidates Supported Victorious

2   •   Candidates Supported Defeated

"THE WALL"

18 Billion   •   Dollars Requested of Congress (U.S., not Mexican) For "The Wall"

0   •   Miles Of "The Wall" Built

0   •   Dollars Paid By Mexico For "The Wall"

WHAT A TEAM!

3	•	Billionaires in Cabinet
1	•	Attorney General Recusals
1	•	Special Counsels Appointed
1	•	FBI Directors Fired
1	•	FBI Directors Threaten to Resign
1	•	White House Counsel Threaten to Resign
22	•	Senior Administration Officials Resigned or Fired (Of 64 – 34% turnover)
256	•	Senior Administration Positions Unfilled

THE FRANCHISE

3 Million	•	More Votes Hillary Clinton Received in 2016 Election
3 Million	•	Fraudulent Voters Claimed in 2016 Election
0	•	Fraudulent Voters Found
1	•	Presidential Commissions Established (Voter Fraud)
1	•	Presidential Commissions Dissolved (same)

THIS LAND IS OUR LAND

1,200,000	•	Acres of Bear Ears National Monument Reduced
26	•	New Areas of Continental Shelf Opened To Oil and Gas Drilling (Florida excepted)

WORKIN' 9 TO 5

111	•	Vacation Days Taken
75	•	Golf Outings
117	•	Days Spent At Trump Properties
4	•	Average Hours Per Day Scheduled as Unspecified "Executive Time"

934+	•	Tweets (trumptwitterarchive.com)
18	•	Interviews on FOX
1	•	Interviews on NBC, MSNBC, ABC and CBS each
0	•	Interviews on CNN
1	•	Press Conferences (v. Obama 7)

THE PETTY

184	•	People, Place and Things Insulted on Twitter
13	•	"Nicknames" Bestowed On Enemies
73	•	Claims of "Fake News"
? [25]	•	"Alternative Facts" Posited

TAX MAN

5.5 Trillion	•	Dollars Claimed in Tax Cuts
1.5 Trillion	•	Actual Dollars in Tax Cuts
11.3	•	Billion Fewer Dollars Federal Reserve Paid to Treasury in Stimulus Profits [2017 Trump $80.2B v. 2016 Obama $91.5B]
1 Trillion	•	Dollars – 2017 Deficit
20 Trillion	•	Dollars – National Debt
440 Billion	•	Dollars U.S. Needs To Borrow First Quarter 2018

REGULATIONS

57,050	•	Pages Added to Federal Register (6,955 fewer than Obama – 9.9%)
58	•	Executive Orders (30% more than Obama 41)
860	•	Pending Regulations Claimed Killed/Stalled
469	•	Pending Regulations Actually Withdrawn

---

[25] Too numerous to count.

JUDGES AND LAWYERS

1	•	Supreme Court Justice Appointed
41	•	Federal Judgeships Vacant
23	•	Federal Judges Appointed
73	•	Federal Judges Nominated
91	•	% of Federal Judges Nominated Who Are White
81	•	% of Federal Judges Nominated Who Are Male
37	•	Nominees From Big Law Firms

TALE OF THE TAPE

6'3"	•	Claimed 2018 Height
6'2"	•	Actual 2017 Height
239 lbs.	•	Claimed 2018 Weight (1 lb. below obese]
TBD	•	Actual Weight

ART OF THE DEAL

0	•	Deals Made With Adversaries (Domestic and/or Foreign)
1	•	Federal Government Shutdowns
3	•	International Agreements Renounced

ALL ABOUT THE BENJAMINS

| 14 | • | % Point Reduction in Taxes For Corporations (21% from 35%) |
| 0-4 | • | % Point Reduction in Taxes For Individuals |

WAR AND MORE WAR

| 3,600 | • | More Troops in Afghanistan (11,000 Trump v. 8,400 Obama) |

| 1,500 | • | More Troops in Syria (2,000 Trump v. 500 Obama) |
| 3,730 | • | More Troops in Iraq (8,992 Trump v. 5,262 Obama) |

THE ECONOMY

23,000	•	Solar Industry Jobs Loss Expected Due To New Tariff
4.1	•	% Unemployment Rate (4.8% in 2016 – <u>no</u> difference in Trend)
3	•	% Promised Growth in GDP
2.3	•	% Actual Growth in GDP (1.5% in 2016 – <u>no</u> difference in Trend)
185,000	•	Fewer New Jobs Created in 2017 (2,055,000 - Trump) than in 2016 (2,240,000 - Obama)

THE 99%

345	•	Mass Shootings in U.S.
987	•	Killed In Police Shootings [up from 963 in 2016]
917	•	Hate Groups in U.S. [up from 892 in 2016]
260,000	•	Hate Crimes

"FOREIGNERS"

46,000	•	Haitians Refugees Ordered Deported – All of Whom Claims Have AIDS
2,500	•	Nicaraguan Refuges Ordered Deported
200,000	•	Salvadoran Refuges Ordered Deported
0	•	Persons Deported From Predominately White Countries
800,000	•	Dreamers Left In Immigration Limbo After Ending DACA
2	•	International Travel Bans Issued
54	•	Nations Called "shithole countries"

186,000,000	•	Nigerians Claimed To Live "In Huts" [N.B., 2016 Population of Nigeria is 186,000,000 – 50% urban]

DRAINING THE SWAMP

3.3 Billion	•	Dollars Spent on Washington Lobbyists (10% > than 2016)

RATS…

38	•	House Republicans Retiring
10	•	Days – Shortest Term of Administration Official (Anthony Scaramucci a/k/a "The Mooch")

JUST WEIRD

2	•	Uses of "covfefe"
130,000	•	Dollars Paid in Hush Money to Porn Star
10	•	Words of Star Spangled Banner Known [out of 80]
0	•	Pieces of Evidence Found of Obama Bugging Trump Tower
TBD	•	Cheeseburgers Consumed (in and out of bed)
6	•	Rolls of Paper Towels Tossed To Homeless Puerto Rican Hurricane Victims
? [26]	•	Superlatives Used About Self
324	•	Claims That Only He Can Solve Problem

HOPE SPRINGS ETERNAL

34	•	% Approval Rating
2	•	U.S. Constitution Provisions That Could Save Us (Art. II and Amendment 25)

---

[26] Too numerous to count, but experts estimate over 500.

Although I have sent a copy of this tally to the White House, I have low confidence that it will be read and zero confidence that it will be well-received and/or appreciated, even if read. Since the inaugural, I have sent him a pocket U.S. Constitution once a week, every week and there is still <u>no</u> evidence he has read it. (<u>The Philadelphia Lawyer</u>, Vol. 80, No. 2, Summer 2017)

If this makes it on "Fox & Friends," Mr. President, <u>please</u>, <u>please</u>, sue me!

I cannot wait to depose you.

After Bob Mueller does, of course.

AFTERWARD

For their support, encouragement, critiques and tolerance, I thank my colleagues on the Editorial Board of <u>The Philadelphia Lawyer</u>. In particular, I am indebted to John Gregory who first encouraged me to write for the magazine and to Steve LaCheen whose works therein I have enjoyed and been inspired by since my earliest days at the bar.

While I take credit for most of the thoughts herein and have strived for accuracy and completeness, I also take full and sole blame for any errors or omissions.

And lastly, I could not have completed any of these works without the tireless support and efforts of my long-time, loyal and outstanding assistant and friend, Patricia Benz, who typed, re-typed and retyped these works.

M. Kelly Tillery
Villanova, Pennsylvania
June, 2018

ABOUT THE AUTHOR

M. Kelly Tillery is a Philadelphia Lawyer, partner in the law firm of Pepper Hamilton LLP. He is a graduate of Swarthmore College and the University of Pennsylvania Law School. A proud single father of a son, Alexander, and two daughters, Erin and Kate, he lives in Villanova, Pennsylvania. tilleryk@pepperlaw.com

"Let there be no mistake, regardless of how accurate or even truthful, I take full responsibility and credit for inviting M. Kelly Tillery to join the Editorial Board of <u>The Philadelphia Lawyer</u> magazine. I knew Kelly, the lawyer, from various associations over the years and had championed the first few articles he submitted to <u>TPL</u> for publication. I was, and remain, a fan of his work. His ability to effortlessly tell a story and make it relevant to the important issues of our time is uncanny. I knew he would be a productive member of the Editorial Board and as his many contributions over the years has so proven. Kelly is not only an excellent writer. He is also a prolific one. To those of us who fret and ponder each word and sentence, Kelly's gift is prose which effortlessly transcends such burdens as it effusively fills each page with a thought-provoking tale. This book is the opportunity for his work to be enjoyed by readers other than members of the Philadelphia bar"

John C. Gregory, Jr.
General Counsel
STREAMLIGHT, INC.

21032691R00162

Made in the USA
Columbia, SC
17 July 2018